Bose and His Statistics

Vignettes in Physics

A Series by G. Venkataraman

Title	Abbreviations
A Hot Story	*A Hot Story*
At the Speed of Light	*Relativity*
Bhabha and His Magnificent Obsessions	*Bhabha*
Bose and His Statistics	*Bose*
Chandrasekhar and His Limits	*Chandra*
Quantum Revolution (3 vols.)	
1. *The Breakthrough*	*QR I*
2. *QED: The Jewel of Physics*	*QR II*
3. *What is Reality?*	*QR III*
Raman and His Effect	*Raman*
Saha and His Formula	*Saha*
The Many Phases of Matter	*Many Phases*
Why Are Things the Way They Are?	*WATT*
The Big and the Small (2 vols.)	
1. *Journey into the Microcosm : The Story of Elementary Particles*	*Volume 1*
2. *From the Microcosm to the Macrocosm : The Fascinating Link between Particle Physics and Cosmology*	

Vignettes in Physics

Bose and His Statistics

G. Venkataraman

Universities Press

Bose and His Statistics

UNIVERSITIES PRESS (INDIA) PRIVATE LIMITED

Registered Office
3-6-747/1/A & 3-6-754/1, Himayatnagar,
Hyderabad 500 029 (Telangana), India
e-mail: info@universitiespress.com

Distributed by
Orient Blackswan Private Limited

Registered Office
3-6-752 Himayatnagar, Hyderabad 500 029 (Telangana), India

Other Offices
Bengaluru, Bhopal, Chennai, Guwahati, Hyderabad, Jaipur,
Kolkata, Lucknow, Mumbai, New Delhi, Noida, Patna, Vijayawada

First published 1992
Reprinted 1993, 1997, 2006, 2010, 2012, 2015, 2017, 2018

ISBN : 978 81 7371 036 0

Cover: The illustration depicts super fluid creep, a phenomenon associated with Bose condensation in liquid helium. See Chapter 7

Frontispiece
Satyendranath Bose

Typeset by
Alliance Phototypesetters, Puducherry 605 013

Printed in India at
Yash Printographics, Noida

Published by
Universities Press (India) Private Limited
3-6-747/1/A & 3-6-754/1, Himayatnagar,
Hyderabad 500 029 (Telangana), India
e-mail: info@universitiespress.com

Contents

Preface

To the adult reader

This book and others in this series written by me are inspired by the memory of my son Suresh who left this world soon after completing school. Suresh and I often used to discuss physics. It was then that I introduced him to the celebrated *Feynman Lectures.*

Hans Bethe has described Feynman as the most original scientist of this century. To that perhaps may be added the statement that Feynman was also the most scintillating teacher of physics in this century.

The Feynman Lectures are great but they are at the textbook level and meant for serious reading. Moreover, they are a bit expensive, at least for the average Indian student. It seemed to me that there was scope for small books on diverse topics in physics which would stimulate interest, making at least some of our young students take up later a serious study of physics and reach for the Feynman as well as the Landau classics.

Small books inevitably remind me of Gamow's famous volumes. They were wonderful, and stimulated me to no small extent. Times have changed, physics has grown and we clearly need other books, though written in the same spirit.

In attempting these volumes, I have chosen a style of my own. I have come across many books on popular science where elaborate sentences often tend to obscure the scientific essence. I have therefore opted for simple English, and I don't make any apologies for it. If a simple style was good enough for the great Enrico Fermi, it is also good enough for me. I have also employed at times a chatty style. This is deliberate. Feynman uses this with consummate skill, and I have decided to follow in his footsteps (whether I have succeeded or not, is for readers to say). This book is meant to be read for fun and excitement. It is a book you can even lie down in bed and read, without going to sleep I hope!

Naturally I have some basic objectives, the most important of which is to stimulate the curiosity of the reader. Here and there the reader may fail to grasp some details, and in fact I have deliberately pitched things a bit high on occasions. But if the reader is able to experience at least in some small measure the *excitement* of science, then my purpose would have been achieved. Apart from excitement, I have also tried to convey that although we might draw boundaries and try to compartmentalise Nature into different subjects, she herself knows no such boundaries. So we can always start anywhere, take a random walk and catch a good glimpse of Nature's glory. Where she is concerned, all topics are 'fashionable'. There is today an unnecessary polarization of the young towards subjects that are supposed to be fashionable. To my mind this is unhealthy, and I have tried to counter it.

This series is essentially meant for the curious. With humility, I would like to regard it as some sort of a 'Junior Feynman Series', if one might call it that. With much love, and sadness, it is dedicated to the memory of Suresh who inspired it.

To the young reader

The name of Satyendranath Bose will live for ever in Physics. You will know why when you read this book. Unfortunately, most people in India have never heard of him. I would not be surprised if most of our scientists also do not know much about him, although they might have heard his name. Indeed, I am prepared to bet that barring a sprinkling of physicists (mostly theorists), many in our physics community too are ignorant about Bose. Even if they have heard of him, it is quite likely that they are not aware of the significance of his work.

Bose made a monumental discovery which should make us all feel proud. I wish to tell you about it, and also to explain why it is important. I hope you would be inspired. Who knows, one day you might yourself make an important discovery!

Acknowledgements

This volume would not have been possible but for invaluable help from Mr. John D. Vincent and Mr. A. Ratnakar in collecting the source material. As earlier, Professor V. Balakrishnan, Professor N. Mukunda and Dr. M. V. Atre went carefully through the draft and steered me away from errors. To all of them my grateful thanks. Mrs. Naga Nirmala rendered useful assistance in converting the rough draft into a publishable manuscript. The friendly cooperation of the publisher is also acknowledged.

G.VENKATARAMAN

1 *Happy New Year*

Satyendranath Bose, Satyen to his friends and S.N. Bose to the scientific world was born on 1 January 1894 in Calcutta. His father Surendranath Bose worked in the Railways. Satyen was the eldest and the only son of his parents. There were six younger sisters.

Great scientists seem to come in two categories—some apparently poor in studies in school, and others with a brilliant record. Einstein is supposed to have been of the former type while Bose belonged to the latter. He did very well in school, especially in mathematics. Once, his maths teacher gave him 110 marks out of 100 because Bose had not only answered all questions correctly, but some of them in more ways than one.

A great national fervour swept Bengal during Bose's childhood and naturally he was very much influenced. India was then under British rule (see Box 1.1). A powerful army was used to maintain control but many great people—writers, poets, novelists, scholars, lawyers and so on—raised their voice in various ways. Everyone wanted to contribute to the Swadeshi movement in some way or the other and, as Bose later remarked, "We wanted to put scientific knowledge to use through technology for the benefit of the people or to contribute to science by intensive study." Bose was not alone in thinking in this manner. Nearly half a century before him there was another great man who thought likewise—Mahendra Lal Sircar. But that is a story in itself (see Box 1.2).

Box 1.1 It suffices to describe one incident which greatly aroused public anger during the days of the British rule, and that is the partition of Bengal. Around the turn of the century, the province of Bengal was very large, comprising not only today's West Bengal but also parts of Bihar and Bangladesh as well. Around 1905, the British partitioned Bengal into two provinces. The people of Bengal strongly resented this, suspecting that the British wanted to weaken the people by dividing them. The popular feeling was that the British were trying to dissipate the Swadeshi movement by this process. Contrary to the result expected by the British, the partition of Bengal infuriated the people even more, and their agitation against the British rulers became violent at times. In a letter to his daughter Indira, Nehru described these events as follows:

> Governments have only one method of meeting an argument or demand which they do not like—the use of the bludgeon. So the Government indulged in repression and sent people to prison, and curbed the newspapers with press laws, and let loose crowds of secret policemen and spies to shadow everybody they did not like ... But repression did not succeed in crushing Bengal ... Finally, in 1911 the British government reversed the partition of Bengal. This triumph put new heart in the Bengalis.

Box 1.2 Mahendra Lal Sircar was born in Calcutta in 1833. After completing school, he joined the Calcutta Medical College and obtained the M.D. degree in 1863, standing first. But his interests ranged far outside medicine. Deeply nationalistic in outlook, he began to think hard about how the country's problems could be solved and came to the conclusion that the only way was through science. So, along with several friends who thought like him, he worked hard to set up a centre for scientific research similar to the Royal Institution in London. This, by the way, is the place where famous men like Faraday, Sir James Dewar and several others had done their pioneering research. After much effort by Sircar, such an organisation was finally created in Calcutta in 1876 and it was named the Indian Association for the Cultivation of Science. The Association soon became a meeting place for those interested in science, and the main activity was lectures. Among those active in giving lectures in mathematical physics was Sir Ashutosh Mookerjee. However, Sircar dreamt that there would be something more to the Association than mere lectures—in other words he dreamt of someone like Faraday who by his brilliant research would inspire and also bring glory to the Association. Unfortunately, nobody was keen on doing research at the Association, and Sircar died in 1904, a very disappointed man.

Sircar's effort was not all in vain. In 1907, C.V. Raman then an officer working in the Government, happened to become aware of the Association and being passionately fond of research, began to spend all his spare time there doing research. For ten years he worked there all by himself (of course ably assisted by an attendant named Ashutosh Dey, popularly known as Ashu Babu) on acoustics and optics. He published his results in well-known journals like *Nature*, the *Philosophical Magazine* and the *Physical Review*. In 1917, Sir Ashutosh Mookerjee had Raman appointed as the Palit Professor in the Calcutta University. Raman's research became even more vigorous since he now began to attract students. Finally in 1928, he discovered the *Raman effect* for which he received the Nobel Prize in 1930.

The Association was originally located in Bow Bazaar Street. In the fifties, it was moved to a more spacious location in Jadavpur by Meghnad Saha, where it is presently located. In 1976, the Association celebrated its centenary. In 1988, there was a National function at the Association to celebrate the birth centenary of Raman. On that occasion a monument was unveiled to be erected later at Bow Bazaar Street to commemorate the discovery of the Raman effect. See also, *Raman and His Effect.*

Bose studied in the Hindu High School in Calcutta and after passing the Matriculation examination in 1909, entered the Presidency College. There were many good teachers in that college, including J.C. Bose (see Box 1.3) and P.C. Ray (see Box 1.4). In college, Bose went through Intermediate (see Box 1.5), B.Sc. and then M.Sc. which he passed in 1915, his subject being "Mixed Mathematics"; today, we would probably call it applied mathematics or mathematical physics. Some of Bose's college mates later became famous themselves, e.g., Meghnad Saha (see Box 1.6) and P.C. Mahalanobis (see Box 1.7). Interestingly, both in B.Sc. and in M.Sc., Saha was Bose's classmate. On both occasions, Bose raced Saha to the first place; Saha came second.

Box 1.3 Sir Jagdish Chandra Bose was perhaps the first Indian to establish an international scientific reputation. He was born in 1858 and, after completing college education in Calcutta, went to England to study medicine. But physics attracted him more and he switched over to it. He returned to India after getting the D.Sc. degree in Physics from the London University in 1896. In Calcutta, Bose was appointed Professor of Physics in the Presidency College, a post reserved for Englishmen at that time. Since he was not an Englishman, Bose was given a lower salary but he protested and refused to draw his pay! The authorities then came to their senses.

Bose did pioneering work in millimeter waves. Several years before Marconi, he generated and transmitted electromagnetic waves through walls. Naturally, Bose became famous after this demonstration. Later, he repeated this experiment in London before a distinguished audience which included Lord Kelvin. In 1917, Bose founded the Bose Institute in Calcutta. His interests now switched to plant physiology, and he used his experience in physics to demonstrate through clever experiments that plants not only lived, but also responded to stimuli.

Box 1.4 Acharya Prafulla Chandra Ray was born in 1861. After completing college education in Calcutta, he went abroad to study at the University of Edinburgh, where he obtained a doctorate degree in chemistry. On return to India, he too joined the staff of the Presidency College.

Ray became famous for his work on mercurous nitrate which until then defied preparation. Later, he spent many years studying the salts of mercury. Ray was promoted to the Professor's post but he moved over to the University as the Palit Professor of Chemistry in 1916.

Like many others of those days, Ray was swept by the nationalist fervour. He dreamt of big chemical industries in India, and himself founded one, the Bengal Chemicals Ltd., which is still in existence.

Satyen Bose was a student of Ray in college. Apparently, Ray used to make young Satyen sit on a stool by his side during the lectures to prevent him from asking difficult questions!

Box 1.5 In those days, the final exam in school was the Matriculation. Following this, one did two years of what was called the Intermediate. Then came B.A. and M.A. or M.Sc. each requiring two years.

Box 1.6 Meghnad Saha was born in a village near Dacca in 1893. He belonged to a family of shopkeepers who were not very rich. Young Saha was keen on studies, and won a scholarship to study in school. But in 1905 when the Governor of Bengal came to Dacca, Saha joined in a protest march (this was the time when feelings were high against the partition of Bengal) and as a result Saha lost the scholarship. Saha then faced many difficulties in completing his school education. In 1911, he joined the Presidency College in Calcutta. After College, Saha tried for a government job but he was disqualified because he had participated in the nationalist movement. Luckily, Sir Ashutosh Mookerjee saved him by offering him a lecturer's job in the University College of Science. Here Saha began his research career and did his famous work on the *Saha ionization formula,* now a cornerstone of astrophysics. In 1923, Saha became the Professor of Physics in Allahabad University. In 1933, he returned to Calcutta to become the Palit Professor of Physics in the University—by that time Raman, who used to be the Palit Professor, had left for Bangalore. Saha was also closely connected with the Indian Association for the Cultivation of Science. In addition, he founded the *Saha Institute of Nuclear Physics*. In later years Saha became deeply involved in politics. He was a member of the Lok Sabha for many years till he died in 1956. See also, *Saha and His Formula.*

Box 1.7 Prasantha Chandra Mahalanobis was born in a well-to-do family in Calcutta in the year 1893. After receiving the B.Sc. degree in physics in 1912, he left for England for further studies. As the result of a chance encounter with a friend in Cambridge, he decided to study mathematics. Later, finding mathematics too abstract, he again switched over to physics.

In Cambridge, Mahalanobis came in contact with the mathematics genius Ramanujan. One day Ramanujan invited Mahalanobis for lunch and while he was cooking, Mahalanobis kept himself busy with a small mathematics puzzle. After working out the solution, Mahalanobis read out the problem to Ramanujan. From the kitchen the latter dictated a continued fraction, and said the first term of that was the solution to the problem Mahalanobis was solving!

After completing the Cambridge Tripos examination in physics, Mahalanobis went to the Cavendish Laboratory of which Rutherford was the head. It was decided that Mahalanobis would work under C.T.R. Wilson (famous for his invention of the cloud chamber). Mahalanobis then returned to India on what he thought was a short vacation. Meanwhile, the First World War broke out and Mahalanobis was grounded in India. This was a turning point because thereafter Mahalanobis stayed in the country, in the process making great contributions to it. Decades later, Homi Bhabha was similarly forced to stay back in India consequent to the outbreak of the Second World War. And like Mahalanobis, Bhabha too made worthy contributions to the nation. See also, *Bhabha and His Magnificent Obsessions*.

Getting back to Mahalanobis, a physics lecturer's job was vacant in the Presidency College since the Englishman holding the job had gone off to fight in the war. Mahalanobis was appointed to that post. Although he was teaching physics (and planned to pursue physics research under Wilson after the war), Mahalanobis became increasingly interested in mathematical statistics and its applications. This led to the founding of the Indian Statistical Institute which has now grown very big with several branches throughout India. Of course, all this was possible because of the excellent research work done by Mahalanobis himself and for which he received international recognition. A favourite of Nehru, he was invited to join the Planning Commission. The Second Five Year Plan was largely his brain child. Mahalanobis died in 1972.

What one should do after college is always a bit of a problem, but in those days it was really acute, especially for those who had studied science. There were no career opportunities in science because the large number of universities and national laboratories we have today did not exist then. So, after college, most students simply forgot about science no matter how much they were interested in it. But some did not, and these were the people who made all the difference to Indian science. C.V. Raman was perhaps the most famous example. He did not bother about a career in science, and entered Government service. But he *did* bother about science, and pursued it as a hobby for nearly ten years. Later, he had the oppor- tunity to make science a full-time career. The man who gave Raman that opportunity was also the one who helped Bose and Saha. That man was Sir Ashutosh Mookerjee. Trained as a lawyer, he later became a judge of the Calcutta High Court. For Indians to be so appointed was very rare in those days which meant that Ashutosh Mookerjee must have been very good at his profession. But he was also keenly interested in science and in fact used to give lectures in mathematical physics during his spare time. I am sure that if a career in science was available to him, Ashutosh Mookerjee would have made his mark in that field also. Instead, he made his contribution to science by encouraging at a crucial juncture, three of the best physicists this country has produced namely, Bose, Saha and Raman.

It all happened as follows: In the early part of this century, Calcutta University did not have a science department of its own and only conducted the M.Sc. exam. To study for M.Sc. one had to go to the Presidency College. Ashutosh Mookerjee was not satisfied with the training given there, nor did he find the facilities adequate. So he decided to do something about it. First he revamped the syllabus, making it more modern. Next, he started a Science Department in the University. It was called the University College of Science, and from this was later born the Saha Institute of Nuclear Physics. He also collected money to create professorships, and thus it was that he appointed Raman as the Palit Professor of Physics. Similarly, P.C. Ray was appointed the Palit Professor of Chemistry. Bose and Saha were made lecturers in the Physics Department.

It is important to have a feel for the state of physics at that time in order to appreciate the contribution of Bose. Physics is the study of natural phenomena and the laws governing them. Initially the subject grew on the basis of the study of phenomena one could directly see and experience. Our senses are not designed to see atoms directly and so until the beginning of this century, most physicists did not bother about explaining natural phenomena in terms of atoms and molecules. Newton's laws, thermodynamics and Maxwell's equations of electricity and magnetism—the great triumphs of classical physics—none of them explicitly involve atoms and molecules. By about the end of the nineteenth century, many people thought that all the major discoveries of physics had already been made, and that all that was left was a mere filling-in of the details. All these astrologers were proved completely wrong because close on the heels of these predictions came a flood of new and momentous discoveries—the electron, radioactivity, X-rays, Planck's law of radiation, relativity, etc.,—which shook physics. A new world—the world of the atom—had been opened, and the rules there were quite different. Newton's laws did not hold, and one was not sure if the wave theory of light was true. Nasty problems kept surfacing, and instead of being delighted with the discoveries, many were puzzled and unhappy. Finally, between 1924 and 1930, a series of important breakthroughs occurred and physics settled down again, though in a new *avatar* (see, *The Quantum Revolution, Part I*). Bose's most important work was done in 1924, forming a part of the new wave.

When Bose did his famous work, he was not trying something radically new like Schroedinger (see Box 1.8) or Heisenberg (see Box 1.9) did around that time. He was merely attempting to rederive Planck's law. This law had been known for well over twenty years and several derivations of it had been already given, including one by Einstein. Bose was not happy with those earlier derivations as there seemed to be something lacking in them. So he set about deriving Planck's formula in his own way; and in the process, he made a revolutionary discovery.

Box 1.8 Erwin Schroedinger was the only child of his parents. His father owned an oil-cloth factory, but was more interested in chemistry, botany and painting. Erwin was born in Vienna in 1887. His early education was by private tuition at home but according to Schroedinger, he learnt more from his father than from his tutor. Later he entered the Gymnasium (equivalent of our high school) where he learnt more of Latin and Greek than science! But Schroedinger discovered the pleasures of mathematics which later influenced him very much. After Gymnasium it was the University, and he received his doctorate in 1910. He served in the army as an officer during the First World War, but even so, found time to read Einstein's papers. After the war, he worked for a while in Vienna where he did some experimental work. Soon after marriage in 1920, he moved to Zurich in Switzerland to become Professor there. This post was previously held by Einstein. In Zurich, Schroedinger started working on problems connected with the statistical theory of heat. This is not surprising because Schroedinger was influenced by another great Austrian, Ludwig Boltzmann, who had contributed much to the subject. In 1924, de Broglie in France had suggested that matter could behave both like particles as well as waves. In 1925, following the famous paper by Bose (which is the story of this book), Einstein published a sequel, so to speak, predicting Bose condensation (—see Chapter 7) which we now know to be due to quantum interference. Schroedinger recognised that there was something strange here, and wondered whether it could all be said differently. As he later observed, he wanted to "recast it [Einstein's results] in a more pleasing form, to liberate it from Bose's statistics". Thus was born the famous wave mechanics of Schroedinger. You will hear a bit more about it in Chapter 3.

In 1927, Schroedinger went to Berlin to succeed Max Planck as the Professor in the University there. But life became difficult after 1930 when Hitler came to power and started persecuting Jews. So Schroedinger left for England in 1933. It was in that year he was awarded the Nobel Prize for Physics along with Dirac. In 1939 he moved on to Ireland, where he spent seventeen years. After the Second World War, Austria tried hard to persuade Schroedinger to return; even the President of Austria personally tried to convince Schroedinger. At first Schroedinger refused because Austria was then under Soviet control but when Austria became free, he returned (in 1956). He died in January 1961.

Box 1.9 Werner Heisenberg was born in Germany in 1901. His father was a Professor of Greek in the University of Munich. After completing school, young Werner entered the Munich University in 1920 to study physics under the great Arnold Sommerfeld. In 1923, he went to Gottingen to work under Max Born. Heisenberg then went on a Rockefeller grant to Copenhagen to spend some time in Niels Bohr's institute. While there, he had an attack of hay fever and to recuperate, he went to a place called Helgoland. It was there that he wrote his first paper on quantum mechanics. He tackled the problem of calculating the energy levels of atomic oscillators. His method was daringly original and yielded good results but Heisenberg was not sure if it meant anything and wondered if he should publish his results or "throw it into the flames". Luckily, he showed his manuscript to Max Born who recognising it to be important had it sent to *Physikalische Zeitschrift*. Eight days later, Born noted that Heisenberg's so-called new rules really corresponded to matrix algebra. Thus the mechanics introduced by Heisenberg was called matrix mechanics. Later he discovered the uncertainty principle. For all this he won the Nobel Prize in 1932.

During the Second World War, Heisenberg worked on problems of nuclear energy in Germany and so he was wanted by the American army. When American troops entered Germany he was picked up and interned in England for about a year. After he was released, Heisenberg returned to Germany and helped to build up German physics again. Although Heisenberg is best remembered for his work on quantum mechanics, it must be mentioned that he is also the father of the quantum mechanical theory of magnetism.

We start our story of Bose's discovery from the year 1917. Along with Saha, Bose had just become a lecturer in the University College of Science of Calcutta University. Their duties mainly involved teaching but as Bose later said, "When we began to teach, we had to do things more seriously. We had to try to do something original." Bose and Saha therefore decided to spend some time on research, besides teaching. Research cannot be done in a vacuum. One needs ideas, and to get ideas Bose began to read books—not cheap textbooks but books written by masters like Gibbs (see Box 1.10) and Planck (see Box 1.11). In those days, much of the scientific literature appeared in French and in German, and so one had to learn those languages if one wanted to be up-to-date. Languages came easily to Bose. He not only picked up enough to understand the books, he even began to translate poems from European languages into Bengali!

Box 1.10 Willard Gibbs is one of the great physicists of America who lived in the last century. He was born in 1839. A very bright student, he took up the study of engineering in college. In fact, he was the first person in America to get a Ph.D. in engineering. That was in the year 1863. He then spent a few years in Europe where his interest shifted to physics. In 1871 he was appointed Professor of Mathematical Physics at Yale University (founded, by the way, by a former Governor of Madras). For the first nine years, Gibbs received no salary but that was no problem since Gibbs had money of his own. It was during this period that he did his monumental work on thermodynamics and statistical mechanics. He died in 1903.

Box 1.11 Max Planck was born in Germany in 1858. He attended school in Munich and later studied at the University of Berlin where his teachers included famous people like Helmholtz and Kirchhoff (about whom you will hear more in Chapter 3). After getting his degree, Planck returned to Munich, worked as a teacher for a while in Kiel and finally went back to Berlin in 1889 when Kirchhoff died and the professorship fell vacant. As I shall describe in Chapter 3, Planck made his most famous discovery in 1900, ushering in the quantum era. For his discovery, he received the Nobel Prize in 1918. From 1930 onwards he was the President of the Kaiser Wilhelm Society of Berlin which, after the Second World War, has been renamed the Max Planck Society. Planck stayed in Germany during the War and tried to prevent injustice to Jews. His son was arrested in 1944 for participating in the secret plot against Hitler, and was executed. Planck also lost his home due to bombing by Allied aircrafts. He spent his last years in Gottingen. He died in 1947. Today there is a chain of Max Planck Institutes all over Germany, devoted to topics ranging from astrophysics to metallurgy.

Advanced books by great masters were not available in the library of Calcutta University. But Bose and Saha learnt of Dr. Bruhl in the Bengal Engineering College who had personal copies of many such books. Dr. Bruhl was from Austria. He received his doctorate in botany and as he was not keeping well, he was advised to go to a country with a warmer climate. So he came to India to study Indian plants. While in Calcutta he got married and a job became necessary. This is how he became a teacher in the Bengal Engineering College. Though he was trained only in botany, Bruhl did a good job of teaching engineering physics and in running the practical classes. This was partly because of the excellent set of books he had, and which Bose and Saha now started borrowing.

Bose always believed that to learn a subject, one must go to the source, i.e., the works of the masters. While he himself could read their works in French and German (if they happened to be in those languages), for the benefit of others who might not know those languages, he decided to translate some of the important papers into English. This was a good way to learn both the language and the subject; two birds with one stone kind of thing. And thus it was that he started translating papers on relativity; the collection was later published by the Calcutta University. Now Einstein (who gave us the theory of relativity and who wrote his papers in German) had given the English translation rights to Methuen in England. When they heard about the translation Bose was bringing out, they tried to prevent the Indian publication. Fortunately, Einstein intervened and said that he had no objection as long as Bose's book was for circulation only in India.

In 1921, the Dacca University was started. Today, Dacca is the capital of Bangladesh but in those days it was a part of the Province of Bengal. Dr. Hartog, the Vice Chancellor of Dacca University, wanted to build good departments and selected Bose as a Reader in the Physics Department. This was necessary as the existing Professor wasn't all that good. His name was Mr. Jenkins about whom Bose says:

> He was a clever man but not of any eminence whatsoever; nor had he done any research work. He had been a Professor of Physics in the old Dacca College and when the University was created they took him. He was from Cambridge. He belonged to the Indian Educational Service and was just passable in physics. His special qualification was that he was a good football player and with that merit he was appointed to the professorship of physics.

Having a white skin seemed to matter more than anything else in those days. Of course, many of the Englishmen occupying high positions in India were personally very nice people, and about Jenkins, Bose says, "He was a young man of my age, about 27 years. He was a nice and companionable person, and did not quarrel; he wanted to be on good terms with Indians."

Bose was not just reading and translating. He was always on the lookout for unsolved problems, which is what research is all about, i.e., solving unsolved problems. And once one solves a new problem, one publishes the result, provided of course the result is important. Bose and Saha managed to publish a paper within a year of being appointed lecturers, the topic of the paper being the kinetic theory of gases. The paper appeared in the prestigious scientific journal the *Philosophical Magazine* published in England. In 1919 Bose had two small papers published in the *Bulletin of the Calcutta Mathematical Society*, and in 1920 he had a couple more in the *Philosophical Magazine*. All this was good work no doubt, but not earth shaking.

Sometime in March 1924, Saha visited Dacca which was his hometown. Naturally he called on his old friend Bose, and sure enough they began to talk physics. Bose told Saha that he was trying to teach Planck's law of radiation in class but was not at all satisfied with the derivations available in the literature. Saha in turn drew the attention of Bose to some more recent work by Einstein and by Pauli (see Box 1.12). About the latter paper Bose subsequently recalled:

> What seemed to be happening in Pauli's work was that in order to apply the quantum condition, you had to know exactly what was going to happen afterwards. So there were certain difficulties, and Saha pointed them out to me.

Box 1.12 Wolfgang Pauli was born in Vienna in 1900. His father was a Professor of Chemistry and had the same name. So the son was called Wolfgang Pauli Jr. At school, Pauli excelled in mathematics, and quickly became familiar with Einstein's general theory of relativity which at that time was quite new and hardly understood. It is said that Pauli secretly read Einstein's papers during dull class hours! After finishing school, Pauli went to Munich to study theoretical physics under Arnold Sommerfeld. At that time, the famous mathematician Felix Klein was preparing an encyclopedia of mathematical sciences, and he asked Sommerfeld to contribute an article on Einstein's theory of relativity. Sommerfeld gave that job to Pauli who at that time was barely twenty years old. Pauli returned the compliment by writing a masterly article which even today is considered an excellent introduction to relativity. Pauli's famous work was of course his *exclusion principle*, for which he received the Nobel Prize in 1945. Pauli was also the first to recognise the existence of a tiny particle emitted in β-decay, the *neutrino*. For a while there was a doubt whether such a particle really existed, but it was set to rest when Reines and Cowan actually detected the neutrino in experiments.

Pauli was a terror to his students. He was a sharp thinker and so people used to go to him for comments about their work. In a few instances, people who came up with brilliant ideas abandoned them because of Pauli's disapproval, only to find someone else scooping them up later and even winning great honours. Pauli died in 1958.

And so it was that early in 1924, Bose rederived Planck's law in his own way, in the process introducing an entirely new idea into physics. One does not quite know whether Bose was aware at that time of the full significance of his work. Certainly he did not elaborate on it in his paper. It is therefore often said that he just stumbled on to an important discovery. On the other hand, could it be that he was too hesitant to advertise radical ideas? Anyway, as usual, Bose sent his paper to the *Philosophical Magazine* for publication; but this time they turned it down. Bose was disheartened, because he was convinced that his derivation was more logical than all the earlier ones. Suddenly he got the idea of sending the paper to Einstein in Berlin with a request to have it translated into German and to have it published in the German journal *Zeitschrift fur Physik*. He wrote:

PHYSICS DEPARTMENT.
Dacca University.

Dated, the 4th June 1924.

Respected Sir. I have ventured to send you the accompanying article for your perusal and opinion. I am anxious to know what you think of it. You will see that I have tried to deduce the coefficient $\frac{8\pi\nu^2}{c^3}$ in Planck's Law independent of the classical electrodynamics, only assuming ~~that~~ ~~finite~~ that the ultimate elementary regions in the Phase-space has the content h^3. I do not know sufficient German to translate the paper. If you think the paper worth publication I shall be grateful if you arrange for its publication in Zeitschrift für Physik. Though a complete stranger to you, I do not feel any hesitation in making such a request. Because we are all your pupils though profiting only by your teachings through ~~the~~ your writings. I do not know whether you still remember that somebody from Calcutta asked your permission to translate your papers on Relativity in English. You acceded to the request, the book has since been published. I was the one who translated your paper on Generalised Relativity.

Yours faithfully

S.N. Bose

Physics Department
Dacca University
4 June 1924.

Respected Sir,

I have ventured to send to you the accompanying article for your perusal and opinion. I am anxious to know what you think of it. You will see that I have tried to deduce the coefficient $8\pi\nu^2/c^3$ in Planck's law independent of the classical electrodynamics, only assuming that the ultimate elementary regions in the phase-space has the content h^3. I do not know sufficient German to translate the paper. If you think the paper worth publication I shall be grateful if you arrange for its publication in *Zeitschrift fur Physik*. Though a complete stranger to you, I do not feel any hesitation in making such a request. Because we are all your pupils though profiting only by your teachings through your writings. I do not know whether you still remember that somebody from Calcutta asked you permission to translate your papers on Relativity in English. You acceded to the request. The book has since been published. I was the one who translated your paper on Generalised Relativity.

Yours faithfully,

S.N. Bose.

You might be wondering why Bose himself did not translate his paper into German. The answer is simple. Bose certainly knew enough German to translate from that language into English. The reverse is always harder, which was the reason for his seeking help from Einstein. Einstein was already a world figure at that time and it really required a lot of courage for an unknown person to write to a supremo like Einstein. The latter was very kind and did not straightaway dismiss Bose as a crank. Celebrities invariably receive a lot of mail and since much of it is trash, there is the danger of genuine letters being ignored along with those containing nonsense. Luckily for Bose, Einstein read his paper carefully, translated it, and had it published. What is more, he added a comment that Bose's paper was important. Soon he followed it up by extending Bose's work. All this changed Bose's destiny, from being an obscure physicist to one with a place in the Hall of Fame. In the next few chapters, we shall concentrate on the physics underlying Bose's discovery, its significance and some of the fallout that occurred.

2 *Vacancies And Occupation*

When I was a student in college, I used to enjoy problems in algebra involving permutations and combinations. A typical one would be: There are so many boys in a class and they want to have a group photograph; but there are not as many chairs as there are boys. In how many ways can the group be arranged for the photo, given the number of chairs?

This problem is a special case of a very general one illustrated in Fig. 2.1 where there are N objects which have to be organised into n lots.

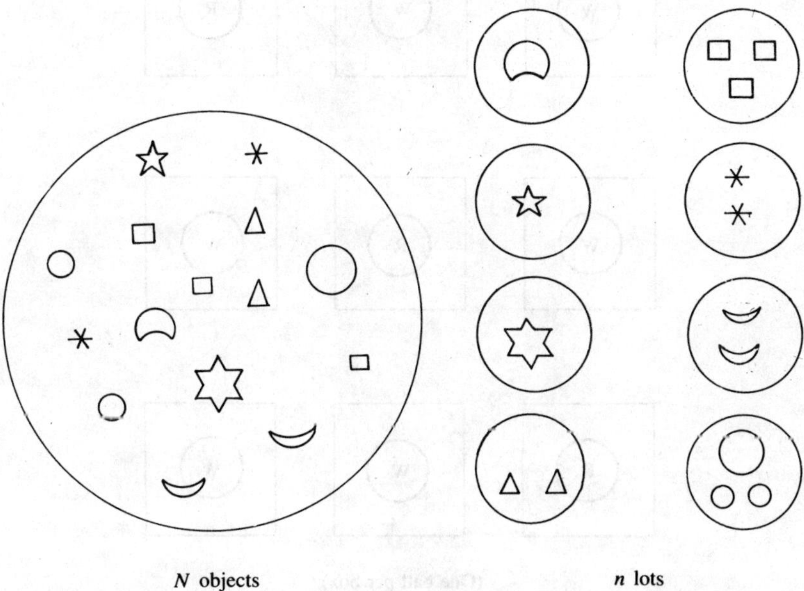

Fig. 2.1 Shown here is an assorted collection of N objects divided into n lots. This is a very general problem, seemingly without any meaning. However, when specialised, the problem starts becoming meaningful. For example, the objects could all be balls and the lots could be boxes. Then the problem is one of organising the balls into boxes. More of this as we go along.

And the question is: In how many ways can this (objects into lots) be done? From this general problem many special cases can be derived, the group photo problem being one example. More about all this in Chapter 4.

Ever seen billiards? The game is played with one red ball and two white ones. I have always been fascinated by this game because many of the things we learn about collisions in mechanics come alive. I have also admired the balls—they look so perfect.

Let us say we take these three balls and try to arrange them in three boxes. How many different arrangements can we have? I say, "Only those in Fig. 2.2." You think for a while and say, "Objection! There are two white balls and for every arrangement you have shown, there is another in which the white balls are swapped."

You have a point but it all depends on what assumption we make about the white balls. If, for example, we make tiny scratches on them so that we

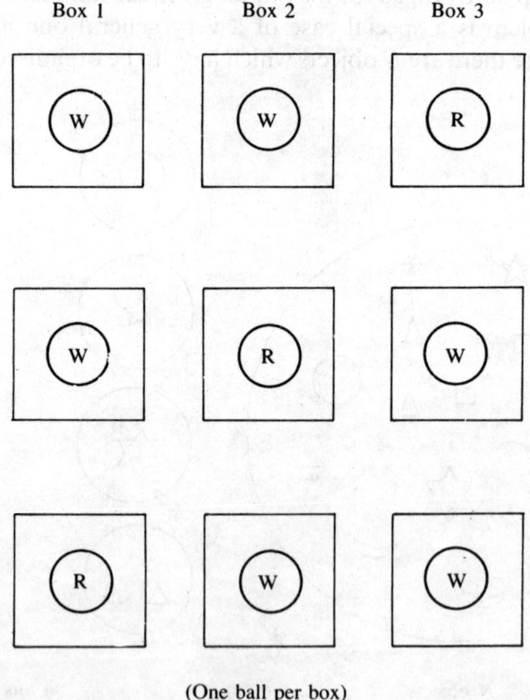

Fig. 2.2 This is an elementary exercise in which we try to distribute one red ball and two white balls amongst three boxes, with one ball per box. The different possible arrangements are shown. Of course, I have assumed that the two white balls cannot be told apart. If they can be distinguished, then one would get three more arrangements.

can tell the two white balls apart, then we can say which white ball occupies which slot and your argument would be correct. On the other hand, if there is no way we can tell the two balls apart, then the only *distinct* arrangements possible are the ones shown in Fig. 2.2. In short, the question boils down to: Are the two white balls distinguishable or indistinguishable?

In physics, when objects are *indistinguishable*, we say they are *identical*. We deal with all kinds of elementary particles in modern physics—electrons, protons, neutrons, mesons of all sorts, neutrinos, photons . . . There is a bewildering zoo, but that is another story. It is interesting that while one can certainly distinguish between an electron and a proton, all electrons are identical, all protons are identical, all neutrons are identical . . . Get the idea? So in short, *all elementary particles of the same species are identical*. This has important consequences.

Let a particle of a given species have a certain set of allowed energy levels, say as in Fig. 2.3. Depending on the circumstances, our particle can occupy any one of these levels. Suppose that instead of just one particle

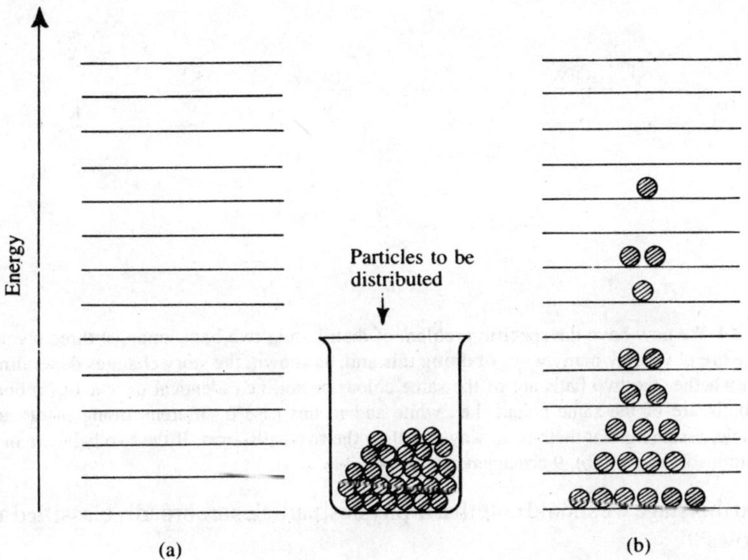

Fig. 2.3 While studying gases and liquids, we always deal with a large number (N) of identical particles and we often want to know what sort of energies this group of particles can have. A simple way of dealing with this problem is to first figure out what sort of energy levels or states *one* particle can have. Suppose it is like in (a). Next we assume that *every* particle in this group of N particles has the *same* choice of states or levels. The problem now is to distribute the N particles amongst these available levels. One scenario is shown in (b). Is such a scenario actually possible for the group of particles under consideration? This is where the different types of statistics come into the picture.

we have N of these and that each one of these has the same choice of energy levels to occupy. In how many ways can these N particles be distributed among these energy levels?

We must now be very careful! Let us be specific and say that there are three levels as in Fig. 2.4. There are also two "baskets", one containing identical red balls R and the other containing identical white balls W. Note the qualification, identical. We are asked to pick two balls at a time and distribute them among the three levels. The different ways in which this can be done are shown in the figure. In picking two balls, we could choose one R and one W or both W or both R. Figure 2.4 shows that there is a clear difference, depending on whether both the balls are of the same colour or not, i.e., identical or distinguishable.

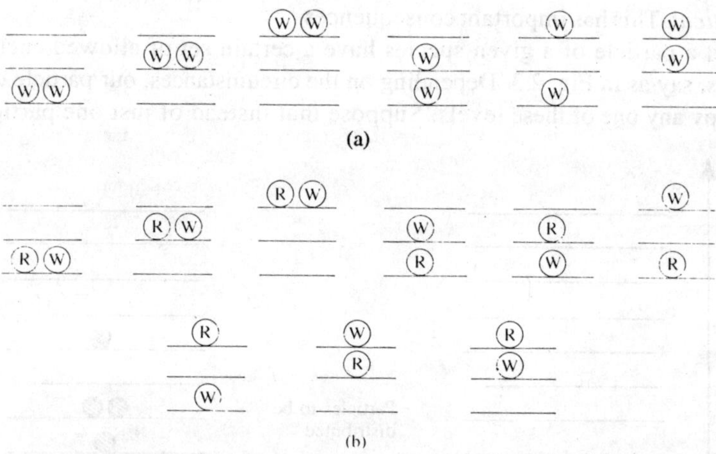

Fig. 2.4 We now have the specific problem of distributing two balls amongst three levels. There are obviously many ways of doing this and, as shown, the story changes depending upon whether the two balls are of the same colour or not, i.e., identical or not. In (a) both the balls are of the same colour, i.e., white and in this case 6 different arrangements are possible, assuming that there is no way of telling the two balls apart. If the two balls are of a different colour as in (b), 9 arrangements are possible.

At this stage we should note that in physics, particles are broadly classified as follows:

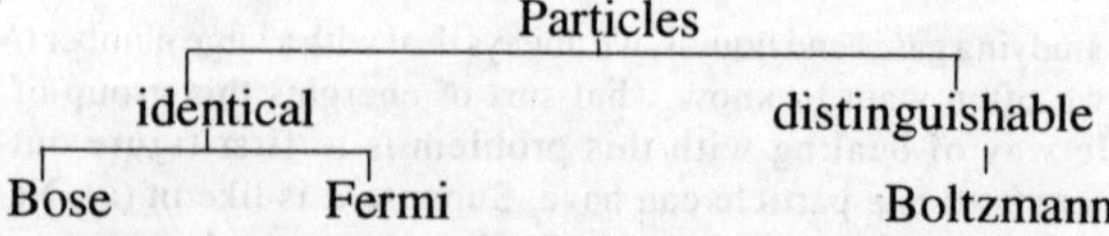

See Appendix to this chapter, for some examples of Bose and Fermi particles, also called *Bosons* and *Fermions* respectively.

So there are three categories, named after famous physicists, one of whom, notice, is none other than Bose. What is the difference in the behaviour of these types of particles? Answer: The way in which they can be packed into available states/levels—see Fig. 2.5. What emerges is that *any number of identical Bosons can occupy a given (quantum) state but no more than one Fermion can occupy a given state.*

What about the poor Boltzmann particles? Why no mention of them above? That is because all elementary particles in Nature are either Bosons or Fermions (at least those known so far). There are *NO* particles of the so-called Boltzmann type. Why then did Boltzmann invent something which today we say has nothing to do with reality? Ah, there is a good reason. You see, both Fermions and Bosons *behave like* Boltzmann particles under certain conditions, and until this century, the phenomena which people studied corresponded mostly to such conditions. These

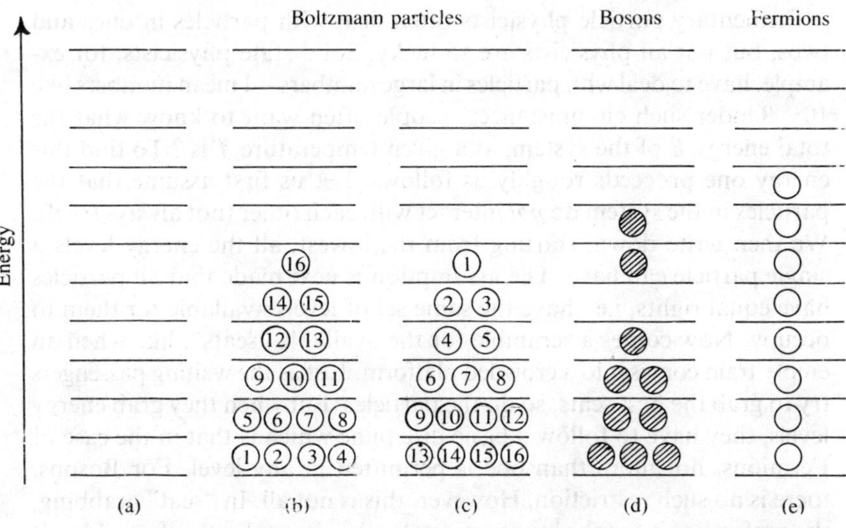

Fig. 2.5 The purpose of this figure is to show how, given the same choice of energy levels, say as in (a), the Boltzmann, the Bose and the Fermi particles can distribute themselves. The Boltzmann particles are distinguishable, and there is no restriction about how many of them can be accommodated in an energy level. (In practice, there might be problems with energy supply but that does not concern us here.) The Bosons also have a lot of freedom and can in principle all crowd into a given energy level. However, while the shuffling of Boltzmann particles can produce distinct arrangements (compare (b) and (c) where the numbers in successive levels remain the same but the occupancy is by different particles), shuffling of Bosons or Fermions does not produce anything new. The Fermions are very, very reserved, meaning that they don't occupy a level where there is already a fellow. In short, just one particle per level—this is the Pauli exclusion principle, which I shall formally introduce you to in Chapter 5.

Caution: There are no Boltzmann particles in Nature. However, at high enough temperatures, both Bosons and Fermions behave like Boltzmann particles.

studies therefore did not reveal (in an obvious manner) the existence of either Fermi or Bose particles. In other words, there was no *need* for Boltzmann to invent anything other than what he actually did (more about this in Chapter 4). In a nutshell,

> Bosons and Fermions are the only types encountered so far in the quantum world. They differ in their *distributions*, or, if you like, their statistics. However, both *behave like* Boltzmann particles in the so-called *classical limit*.

I am sure you are thoroughly mystified and dissatisfied! Any number of questions must be crossing your mind: "What are these distributions? Why these distributions, and why not others? What is this classical limit? Where does the work of Bose come into all this?" and so on. Be patient! You will get the answers.

Elementary particle physicists often deal with particles in ones and twos, but not all physicists are so lucky. Solid state physicists, for example, have to deal with particles in large numbers—I mean numbers like 10^{23}. Under such circumstances, people often want to know what the total energy E of the system, at a given temperature T is ? To find this energy one proceeds roughly as follows: Let us first assume that the particles in the system do *not* interact with each other (not always true!). We then write down, starting from the lowest, all the energy levels a single particle can have. The assumption is next made that all particles have equal rights, i.e.,.have the same set of levels available for them to occupy. Now comes a scramble for the available "seats", like when an empty train comes into a crowded platform. Just as the waiting passengers try to grab the best seats, so do the particles. But when they grab energy levels, they have to follow a basic discipline which is that in the case of Fermions, not more than one is permitted in any level. For Bosons, there is no such restriction. However, this is not all. In "seat" grabbing, the preference is for the lower energy levels—lower-berths if you like. It is only when they are occupied that the higher levels are sought.

Using these rules, one would then get a scenario like in Fig. 2.6(a) or 2.6(c), depending on whether one is dealing with Bose or Fermi particles. One can now calculate the total energy E using the following rule: First calculate the energy associated with the occupancy in a given energy level i, i.e., multiply E_i (the energy of the level) by the number n_i of particles occupying that level. Repeat for all the levels in the system and add; this gives E, i.e.,

$$E = \sum_i n_i E_i$$

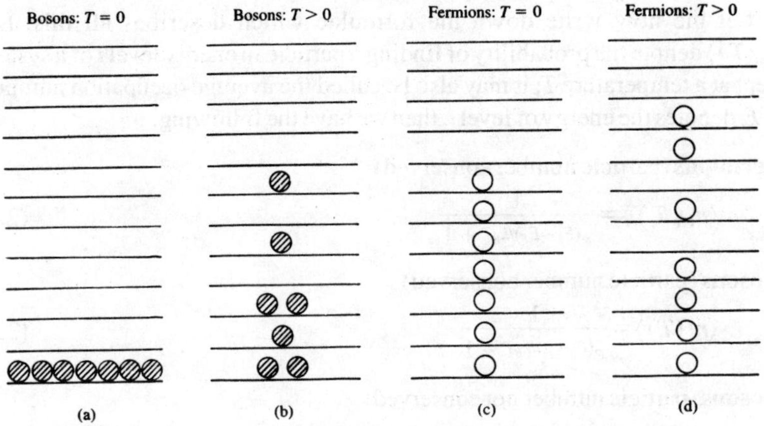

Bosons: $T = 0$ Bosons: $T > 0$ Fermions: $T = 0$ Fermions: $T > 0$

(a) (b) (c) (d)

Fig. 2.6 This figure brings out an important difference between Bosons and Fermions. Compare (a) and (c) which show the occupancy of the available energy levels at the lowest temperature possible, i.e., $T = 0\,^{\circ}\mathrm{K}$. The basic rule of the game is of course that at $T = 0\,^{\circ}\mathrm{K}$, the total energy of the system must be a rock-bottom minimum. Since Bosons don't mind crowding, they achieve this minimum total energy by all of them crowding together into the lowest energy state. The Fermions go along with the idea of keeping the total energy to a minimum, but they must have their single accommodation! This then produces the situation in (c). Scenarios (b) and (d) show what happens at nonzero absolute temperatures. The particles now spread themselves and start occupying levels which they avoided at $T = 0\,^{\circ}\mathrm{K}$. However. Fermions still keep aloof.

where the symbol $\sum_i$ means sum over all the levels *i*.

Figures 2.6 (a) and (c) apply at the absolute zero of temperature. You would naturally wonder: Where on earth does the temperature come into all this? This is what I have to explain next.

To boil water we have to heat it. In general, to maintain a system at a given temperature *T*, we have to place it in contact with a source of heat which is at the required temperature. Such a source is usually called a *heat bath*. When a system of (identical) Fermi particles (like a bunch of electrons say) is placed in contact with a heat bath at a temperature *T*, then some of the particles could pick up energy from the bath to leave the levels they were previously occupying, moving to new levels upstairs which are empty. The higher the temperature, the easier it is for particles to go further up. Thus, when the temperature is greater than (absolute) zero, the picture changes from 2.6(a) to 2.6(b) and from 2.6(c) to 2.6(d) or something like that. What it boils down to is that higher energy levels also have a chance of being occupied at higher temperatures.

Let me now write down the formulae which describes all this. Let $\langle n_i(T) \rangle$ denote the probability of finding a particle in energy level i of a system kept at a temperature T; it may also be called the average occupation number. If E_i denotes the energy of level i, then we have the following:

Fermions (particle number conserved)

$$\langle n_i (T) \rangle = \frac{1}{e^{(E_i - E_F)/k_B T} + 1} \tag{2.1}$$

Bosons (particle number conserved)

$$\langle n_i (T) \rangle = \frac{1}{e^{(E_i - \mu)/k_B T} - 1} \tag{2.2}$$

Bosons (particle number not conserved)

$$\langle n_i (T) \rangle = \frac{1}{e^{E_i / k_B T} - 1} \tag{2.3}$$

Comments:

1. k_B is the Boltzmann constant. You will hear more about it in the next chapter. For the present you may take it as

   $$k_B = R / N_A$$

   where R is the gas constant (remember the law $PV = RT$?), and N_A is the Avogadro n'umber.

2. The number of particles in the system need not always remain the same. If it varies, we say the particle number is not conserved; otherwise it is *conserved*. When one deals with the photon problem (as we shall in later chapters), the number is not conserved and we have to use formula (2.3). On the other hand, if one deals with electrons in metals, the number of electrons is conserved and one has to use formula (2.1). Note, however, that in high-energy physics, the number of Fermions need not be conserved; this is due to particle production/creation.

3. The quantity E_F is called the *Fermi energy*. The quantity (E_F/k_B) has the dimensions of temperature and is called *Fermi temperature* T_F.

4. The quantity μ in formula (2.2) is called the *chemical potential* (see Box 2.1). It is zero when the particle number is not conserved. As you can see, E_F plays the role of chemical potential.

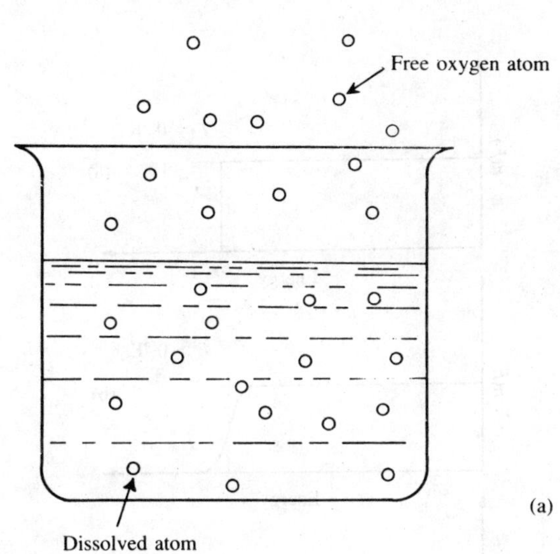

Box 2.1 Thermodynamics is mainly concerned with the exchange of energy (including heat energy) and equilibrium properties. There is no reference to the structure of matter, i.e., one does care about the fact that matter is made up of atoms; only macroscopic behaviour is studied.

The energy of a thermodynamic system may change due to external factors such as a stress, an electric field, etc. These external factors can do work on the system and change its energy content. For example, if the application of a pressure P reduces the volume by an amount dV, then the work done on the system is given by $dW = -PdV$. The term *chemical potential* refers to one such external factor, and is related to the pushing of particles into a system. Consider figure (a). Shown here is a vessel containing say water, with some oxygen atoms dissolved into it. We now wish to push more oxygen atoms into the water; this would mean doing work against a force, and that work per atom is called the chemical potential. More quantitatively, if the number of particles in the system is to be increased by an amount dN, then the work required is given by $dW = \mu dN$, where μ is the chemical potential. It is numerically equal to the work required to push in one extra particle.

Figure 2.7 shows a plot of (2.1) for various temperatures. In the classical limit one can show that

$$\langle n_i(T) \rangle \sim e^{-E_i/k_BT} \tag{2.4}$$

(The symbol ~ means *of the order of*.) Result (2.4) is true both for

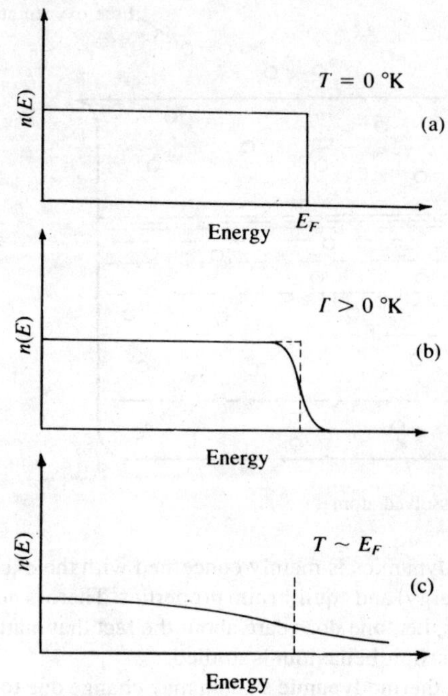

Fig. 2.7 Schematic plot of eqn. (2.1) for various temperatures. At $T = 0$ °K we have a rectangular distribution as in (a). When T is slightly greater than zero, the rectangular distribution is rounded off a bit as in (b) but when T is very large, the Fermi–Dirac distribution (2.1) approaches the Boltzmann distribution (2.4). This is shown in (c).

Fermions and Bosons. Let us make a rough check for Bosons, starting from (2.3). First we rewrite the latter equation as

$$\langle n_i(T) \rangle \sim e^{-E_i/k_BT} / \left(1 - e^{-E_i/K_BT}\right)$$

When T is large (usually this is what the classical limit implies), E_i/k_BT is small. Hence e^{-E_i/k_BT} would be small compared to 1 and can therefore be neglected. Result (2.4) immediately follows. Boltzmann arrived at (2.4) in the last century assuming that particles are *distinguishable*. Moral: when temperature is high, particles *appear* to be distinguishable!

To sum up:

- Elementary particles belonging to a given species are indistinguishable. Some important species are indicated in the Appendix.
- There are only two basic types of elementary particles in Nature, namely Fermions and Bosons.
- The two types obey different distributions—see (2.1) to (2.3).
- In the classical limit, both Fermions and Bosons behave like Boltzmann particles, i.e., they exhibit a distribution similar to what Boltzmann deduced assuming particles were distinguishable.

Undoubtedly you are wondering: "What exactly are these Bosons and Fermions? How can we say which is which?" I am afraid you would have to wait till Chapter 4 for the answers. At this point, I shall merely say that whether an elementary particle is going to behave like a Boson or a Fermion is determined by a property called *spin*. No, spin does not mean what you think. It does not denote spinning like in the case of a spinning cricket or tennis-ball. Rather, it is a name for describing something not known in classical mechanics. It is strictly quantum mechanical in origin. Why then this name? Ah, for that also you have to wait!

Appendix to Chapter 2

Listed below are a few elementary particles and the category to which they belong.

Particle	Spin	Boson	Fermion
Electron	1/2		√
Positron	1/2		√
Neutrino	1/2		√
Proton	1/2		√
Neutron	1/2		√
μ-meson	1/2		√
Omega	3/2		√
π-meson	0	√	
K-meson	0	√	
Photon	1	√	
Graviton	2	√	

Comments:

1. The term spin refers to an intrinsic property called spin angular momentum. It is explained in Chapter 5.
2. As we shall see in Chapter 5, the spin angular momentum of an elementary particle can either be $0, \hbar, 2\hbar, \ldots$ etc. or $\hbar/2, 3\hbar/2, 5\hbar/2, \ldots$ etc. Here $\hbar$ is a fundamental constant which will be introduced in Chapter 3.
3. The numbers (0, 1, 2, . . .), (1/2, 3/2, 5/2 . . .) are referred to as spin quantum numbers. Sometimes the word spin is used for short.
4. Observe from the table that Fermions have half-integer spin while Bosons have integer spin.
5. Besides spin, elementary particles have many other attributes like mass, charge, etc. These are not indicated above.
6. There are several kinds of neutrinos but we have not made a distinction here.
7. Corresponding to particles there are also antiparticles; for example, the positron is the antiparticle of the electron.
8. The particle and the antiparticle belong to the same species, i.e., if one is a Fermion, the other also is.
9. The photon is its own antiparticle.
10. Most of the antiparticles are not shown in the above list.
11. The graviton is the quantum of the gravitational field, just as the photon is the quantum of the electromagnetic field. When we say opposite charges attract, it is all really due to the exchange of photons between the two particles. Likewise, when matter attracts matter due to gravity, it is really due to the exchange of gravitons.

3 *The Photon Story*

3.1 Thirty years that shook physics

Many years ago, the well-known physicist George Gamow wrote a book with the same title as this section. Gamow was referring to the period between 1900 and 1930—you may say starting with the discovery of the electron and ending with Dirac's theory for the electron. In between, our perception of both matter and radiation changed completely, and also that of the Universe. No wonder Gamow chose such a catchy title.

The major events of this momentous period are shown in the chart in Fig. 3.1. It is based on one given earlier by the scientist Abraham Pais, known for his scientific biography of Einstein, *Subtle is the Lord.*

There are two streams in the figure namely, the matter stream and the radiation stream. One cannot really separate matter and radiation, for the two are closely linked (for example, to produce light, we need matter), but at that time, people did tend to concentrate on one or the other. In the end, both streams nicely converged.

Let us wander down the matter stream starting with the German scientist Gustav Kirchhoff, sometimes called the grandfather of the quantum revolution in physics. Kirchhoff was the first to show that spectral lines could be analysed quantitatively. This inspired Balmer (a Swiss school teacher) to arrange the spectral lines of the hydrogen atom into groups and write down nice empirical formulae for their frequencies. The great triumph of Niels Bohr was that he could actually *derive* these formulae using a simple model of the atom. But the model had problems which kept becoming worse till Heisenberg swept all difficulties away with a totally new mechanics, then called *matrix* mechanics. So Newton's mechanics was out, at least as far as atoms were concerned.

We switch now to the radiation stream and once again start with Kirchhoff. He defined what is called a *blackbody*, and wrote down a theorem about the radiation emitted by such a body. During the next few decades, many scientists made careful measurements of the spectrum of radiation

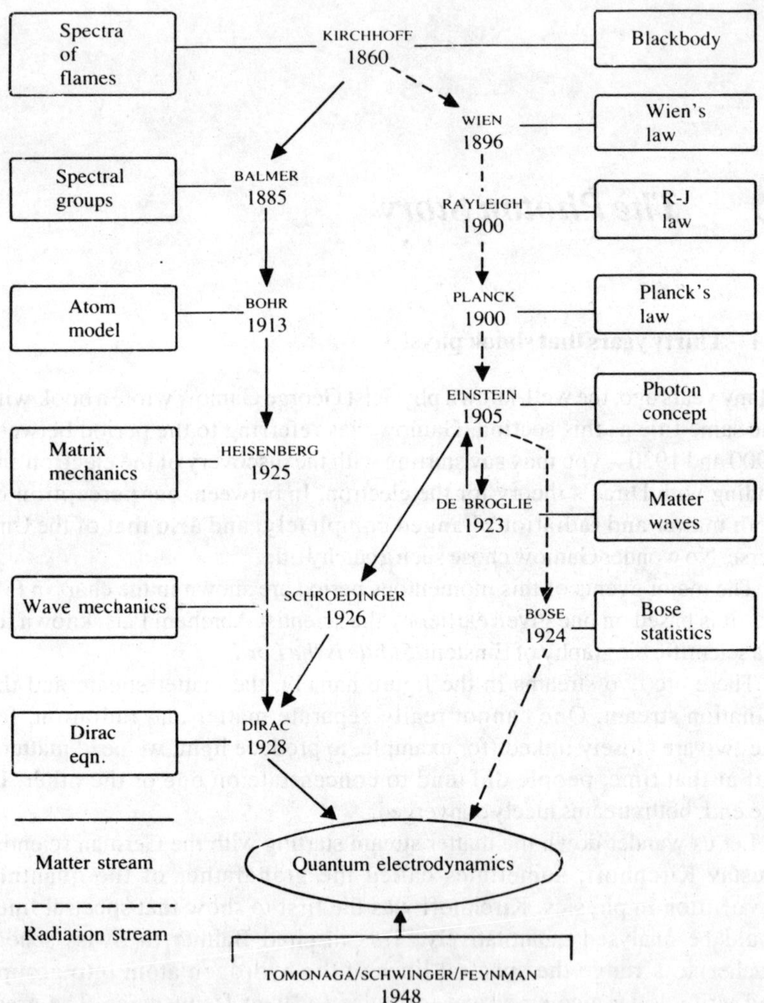

Fig. 3.1 Flow chart showing the evolution of the matter and radiation streams. The events as well as names of persons involved are indicated. The three names shown at the bottom are not referred to in this chapter but are in a later one.

emitted by a blackbody; once the results were available, people also tried to explain them theoretically. But all these efforts failed until in 1900 Planck showed the way with a bold and totally new idea. How- ever, all was not quite well with Planck's derivation of his formula for blackbody radiation. Einstein was one of those who wasn't quite satisfied. In Planck's derivation, the *energy states of matter* (which was responsible for the radiation) *were quantised* but the *energy states of radiation itself were not.* There was thus an asymmetry. Einstein argued that radiation energy also should be quantised, and in this manner revived the corpuscular theory of light, though in a modern form. You might remember that the corpuscular theory of light was first proposed by Newton but was sub- sequently given up because of the difficulty of explaining the interference and the diffraction of light. But now Einstein found that there was no way to explain the photoelectric effect without assigning some kind of a corpuscular nature to light. Actually, *light appeared to have a dual character*, i.e., a wave-like one and a particle-like one. Influenced perhaps by this, de Broglie in France then proposed that *matter too had a dual character.*

This brings us back to the matter stream. Schroedinger built upon de Broglie's ideas to develop his *wave mechanics*, which, like Heisenberg's matrix mechanics, also swept away the difficulties of the Bohr atom model. For a few months it seemed as if there were two theories contending to replace the Bohr model but it was soon proved, by Schroedinger himself, that wave mechanics and matrix mechanics were merely two approaches to the same thing namely, *quantum mechanics*.

Meanwhile in 1923, Einstein's idea that light consisted of particles (now known as photons) received dramatic confirmation with the discovery of the *Compton effect*. Opposition to Einstein's idea which till then was quite strong (the opponents included even Niels Bohr), now completely disappeared. In a sense some goals had at last been reached in the two streams independently, but the linkage between them was still fuzzy. Dirac took care of that between 1928 and 1930, bringing to an end the quest started by Kirchhoff several decades earlier.

3.2 Planck's quantum hypothesis

We now follow the radiation story in slightly greater detail. Consider a body in thermal equilibrium with radiation. A cavity (Fig. 3.2a) provides a good illustration. Let $E(\nu)d\nu$ be the amount of radiation energy emitted per second by unit area of the body (i.e., 1 cm^2) in the frequency interval between the adjacent frequencies ν and $(\nu + d\nu)$. Kirchhoff proved that for a blackbody, $E(\nu)$ must have the form

$$E(\nu) = J(\nu, T) \tag{3.1}$$

where J is a function of only the frequency ν and the absolute temperature T, and does not depend on the particular body at all—see Fig. 3.2 (b). Thus the J

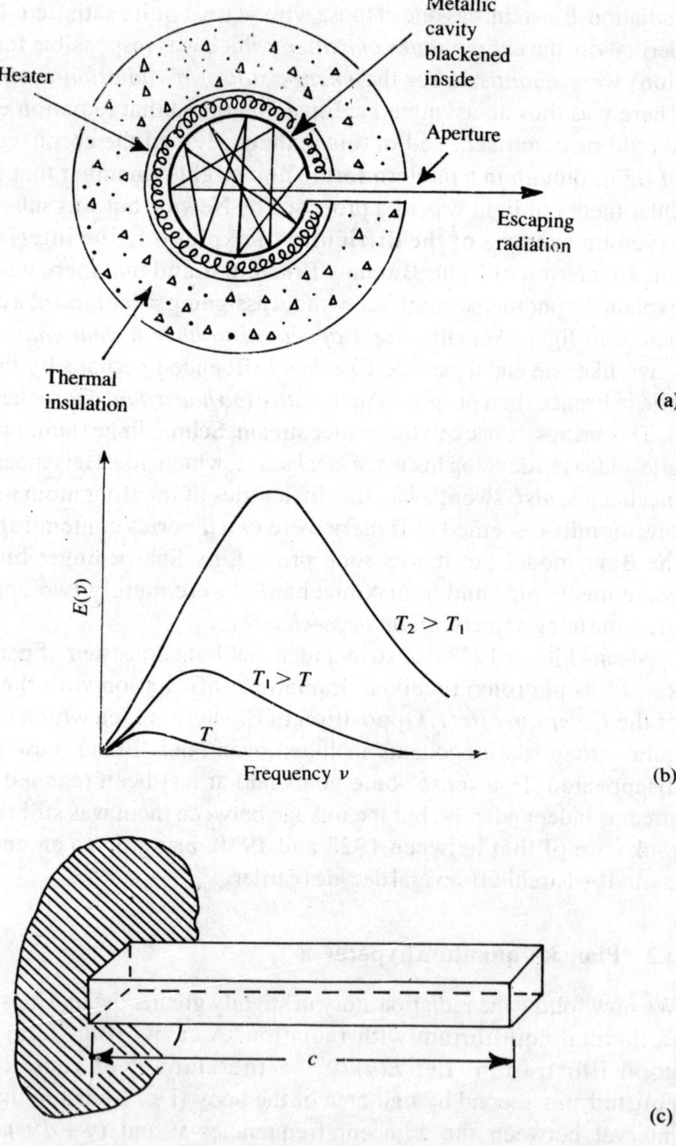

Fig. 3.2 (a) shows a blackbody. It is essentially a hollow spherical çavity suitably insulated and heated to a temperature T, say. The radiation trapped inside has what is called a blackbody spectrum which is shown for various temperatures in (b). To observe this spectrum, radiation must be taken out of the cavity. So an aperture is made, and the radiation allowed to leak out. (c) shows the aperture and the radiation streaming out. If the aperture is opened for one second, the radiation would fill a parallelopiped of length c. The energy in the parallelopiped, between frequencies ν and $\nu + d\nu$, would be $E(\nu)d\nu$.

function is "universal". Kirchhoff challenged experimentalists to determine the form of J so that theorists could attempt to explain it.

It is convenient to write $J(\nu, T)$ as

$$J(\nu, T) = (c/8\pi) \cdot \rho(\nu, T) \tag{3.2}$$

where $\rho(\nu, T)$ is the radiation energy density or the energy per unit vol- ume inside the cavity, and c is the velocity of light (Fig. 3.2c). The name of the game now was to come up with good models for $\rho(\nu, T)$, which would satisfactorily explain experimental results.

Of the many proposals then made only two are remembered now, one due to Wien and the other due to Lord Rayleigh. According to Wien,

$$\rho(\nu, T) = \text{const.}\nu^3 \cdot e^{-\beta\nu/T} \tag{3.3}$$

where β is a constant. This formula is often referred to as *Wien's displacement law*, and for a brief period it seemed OK as it did a good job for *high values of the frequency* ν. But around 1900 there was a break- through in experimental techniques, and accurate results became available in the low-frequency (or infrared) region. It was then found that Wien's law wasn't all that good.

In stepped Lord Rayleigh (Box 3.1). Based on classical physics he deduced that

Box 3.1 Lord Rayleigh was one of the great pillars of classical physics. He was born in England in 1842. As a child he was not healthy. He passed the B.A. examination of the Cambridge University in 1865 as a Senior Wrangler in Maths Tripos—a very difficult feat, which shows Rayleigh's class as well as early promise. Soon after this, Rayleigh suffered an attack of rheumatic fever and was advised to spend some time in a warmer climate. So he went to Egypt, which at that time was under British influence. It was during this period that Rayleigh wrote his famous book on Sound. The remarkable thing is that he did not have access to a library while he wrote this book!

Refreshed by the trip, Rayleigh returned to England in 1873, built a small lab for himself and began to work. He could afford this because of his status as a Lord. In 1879 Cambridge University requested him to become the Cavendish Professor, a position earlier occupied by Maxwell. Rayleigh agreed to the appointment, but only for a limited period of five years. From Cambridge he returned to his hometown.

People normally think of Rayleigh as a mathematical physicist. No question about that, for he *was* an outstanding mathematical physicist. But few seem to know that he was also a very good experimenter. In fact, he was the first to isolate the rare gas argon. Before that, argon was not known. Rayleigh found that the density of nitrogen isolated from the atmosphere was always greater than that of nitrogen prepared in the laboratory by chemical means. Long work eventually led to the discovery and isolation of argon in 1895. Ramsay also went in search of argon after Rayleigh published a note about the anomaly in the density of nitrogen obtained from the two sources. Ramsay isolated other rare gases as well. Both received the Nobel Prize.

Getting back to Lord Rayleigh, it was he who first explained why the sky is blue—it is due to a process we call Rayleigh scattering, and I mention it briefly in Chapter 5. Rayleigh felt the sea is blue because the sky is blue, i.e., due to reflection. Raman wondered about this in 1921 when he was returning by ship from England, and was struck by the deep-blue colour of the Mediterranean sea. Raman showed that the blue colour of the sea also was due to Rayleigh scattering. Further studies on light scattering led him eventually to discover the Raman effect (in 1928).

Rayleigh's papers have been collected together and published. This collected work has inspired many a young student in the old days—like C.V. Raman, K.S. Krishnan (later Director of NPL) and S. Chandrasekhar (see the companion volume *Chandrasekhar and his Limit*).

$$\rho(\nu, T) = c_1 \cdot \nu^2 \cdot T \tag{3.4}$$

where c_1 is a constant. Rayleigh did not evaluate c_1, but that does not matter. More important is the serious flaw in (3.4) which becomes apparent if you see Fig. 3.3. It shows that while Rayleigh's law *does a good job at low frequencies*, it is a disaster at high frequencies. If one took (3.4) seriously and calculated the total energy radiated by the hot body (i.e., taking into account all frequencies), it comes out as infinite which of course is absurd. Rayleigh wasn't very much bothered about this "ultraviolet catastrophe". He did what physicists often do under such circumstances, namely, put a "switch" which removed the undesirable behaviour! With this *cut-off function*, the Rayleigh law became

$$\rho(\nu, T) = c_1\nu^2 \, e^{-(c_2 \nu / T)} \tag{3.5}$$

where c_2 is a new constant. Formula (3.5) predicted a more respectable behaviour compared to the earlier version in (3.4). To complete the story, Lord Rayleigh later computed the constants c_1 and c_2 but made a small error in determining c_1 which was rectified by the famous astronomer Sir James Jeans (who, among other things, wrote an interesting book called *The Mysterious Universe*). Textbooks therefore refer to the corrected formula (3.5) as the *Rayleigh–Jeans law*. In summary, Wien's law worked at high frequencies and Rayleigh's law (3.4) at low frequencies. Nature seemed to be following an intermediate course which was Rayleigh-like at one end and Wien-like at the other.

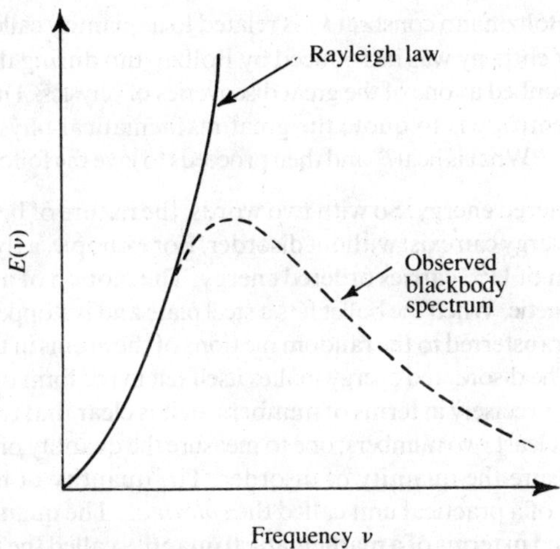

Fig. 3.3 The spectrum predicted by Lord Rayleigh is shown schematically by the solid line while the observed spectrum is shown (again schematically) by the dotted line. As you can see, the Rayleigh formula (3.4) does a good job at low frequencies, but blows up at high frequencies. Remember that barring a constant factor, $E(\nu)$ is the same as $\rho(\nu, T)$.

In October 1900, the German scientist Rubens who was then doing experiments on blackbody radiation paid a visit to Planck. Rubens was accompanied by his wife and it was a social call. But during the conversation Rubens told Planck about his latest measurements in the low-frequency region, adding that the new data did not agree with Wien's law. Planck began to think about the problem (he was not aware of Rayleigh's work), and by the next day he had invented a formula which agreed with Ruben's results. Planck scribbled the formula on a card and posted it to Rubens. The formula was not derived but pulled out of a hat you might say. In modern notation, Planck's formula reads:

$$\rho(\nu, T) = \frac{8\pi h\nu^3}{c^3}\frac{1}{e^{h\nu/k_B T} - 1} \tag{3.6}$$

Here h is a constant now referred to as the *Planck's constant*. I shall frequently use a related constant $\hbar$ (read h cross or h bar); whose value is given by ($h/2\pi$). A word also about k_B, which I promised in the earlier chapter; for convenience, I have put it in Box 3.2.

Returning to Planck and his investigations, formula (3.6) was found to be in excellent agreement with the experiment, both at low as well as high frequencies. Was it a fluke or did it represent a new truth? Planck thought it did. So he spent the next couple of months thinking intensely about it

Box 3.2 The Boltzmann constant k_B is related to a quantity called the *entropy*. The concept of entropy was introduced by Boltzmann during the last century and may be described as one of the great discoveries of physics. The simplest way of explaining entropy is to quote the great mathematical physicist Freeman Dyson. He asks: "What is heat?" and then proceeds to give the following answer.

> Heat is disordered energy. So with two words, the nature of heat can be explained . . . Energy can exist without disorder. For example, a flying rifle bullet or an atom of U^{235} carries ordered energy. The motion of a bullet is of a kind called kinetic. When the bullet hits a steel plate and is stopped, the energy of motion is transferred to the random motions of the atoms in the bullet and in the plate. The disordered energy makes itself felt in the form of heat . . . We measure heat precisely in terms of numbers . . . it is clear that to specify heat we must use at least two numbers; one to measure the quantity of heat and the other to measure the quantity of disorder. The quantity of heat is measured in terms of a practical unit called the *calorie* . . . The quantity of disorder is measured in terms of a mathematical quantity called the *entropy*.

Boltzmann gave us a method for calculating the entropy of a thermodynamic system. In modern language it can be reduced to the formula

$$S = k_B \log_e W$$

Here S is the entropy, and W a quantity related to the random motions. Boltzmann also gave a method for arriving at W. Once W is known, the entropy can be calculated using the above formula. The constant k_B in the above formula is referred to as the Boltzmann constant. Interestingly, this constant was first introduced by Max Planck who also gave it the name we now know it by.

Boltzmann's life ended in a tragedy. Practically single-handed, he developed the kinetic theory of atoms. Some people who did not believe in atoms attacked Boltzmann viciously. Unable to bear the hurt, Boltzmann committed suicide by jumping into the Adriatic Sea, not far from the place where the famous International Centre for Theoretical Physics founded by Abdus Salam is now located. The equation given above now adorns his grave.

and by December 1900, he was able to give a derivation—a great Christmas present to the world of Physics! The chain of ideas underlying Planck's reasoning is shown in the chart in Fig. 3.4, which I shall now explain.

Planck started by supposing that the radiation filling the cavity is produced by material (atomic) oscillators in the walls of the cavity. Not a bad assumption, because by then the electron had been discovered and the Dutch physicist Lorentz had visualised atoms with electrons inside them behaving as oscillators. (Bohr changed that picture later, but that is another story.) The electron experiences acceleration during the oscillation and according to Maxwell's equations of electromagnetism, an

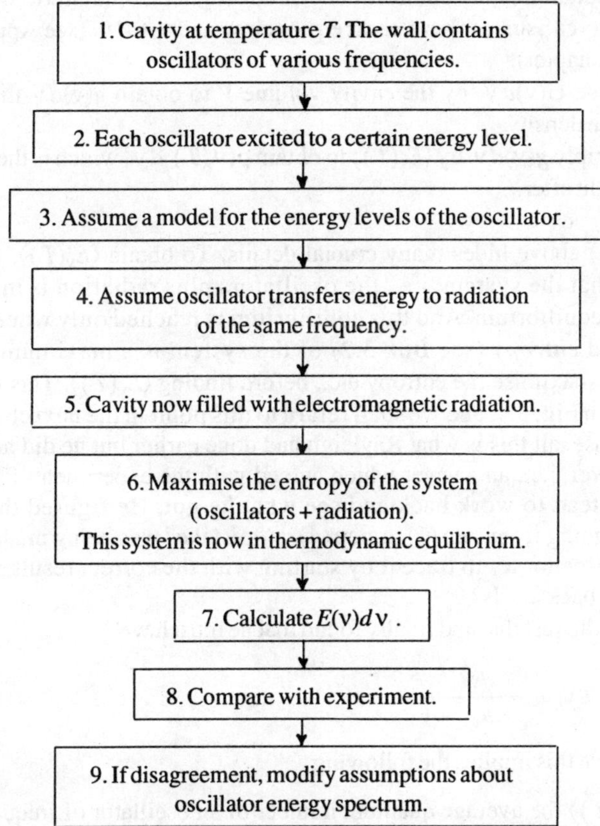

Fig. 3.4 This chart shows the line of reasoning followed by Planck when he derived his formula. While most of the steps are explained in the present section, step 6 is referred to in section 3.3. As you progress through this book, it would be useful for you to periodically come back to this flow sheet. Hopefully your understanding of the radiation problem would then improve and lead to a better appreciation of how Planck went about his business.

accelerated charge would radiate. This is how radiation is supposed to be emitted by the wall of the cavity.

OK, so there are oscillators (in the cavity wall), and an oscillator of frequency ν transfers its energy to an electromagnetic wave of the same frequency. Therefore, to find the energy density in the cavity between frequencies ν and $\nu + d\nu$, all one had to do was the following:

1. Find the *average* energy at temperature T, of an oscillator of frequency ν. Call this quantity $\langle E_\nu(T) \rangle$.

2. Calculate $G(\nu)d\nu$ thenumber ofmodésofelectromagnetic waves the cavitycansustainbetweenfrequenciesν and $\nu + d\nu$ (see Appendix to this chapter).
3. Divide $G(\nu)d\nu$ by the cavity volume V to obtain $g(\nu)d\nu$ the normal mode density.
4. Multiply $g(\nu)d\nu$ by $\langle E_\nu(T)\rangle$ to obtain $\rho(\nu, T)\ d\nu$, which is the quantity sought after.

Step (1) above hides many crucial details. To obtain $\langle E_\nu(T)\rangle$, one must assume that the system, i.e., the oscillators plus radiation is in thermodynamic equilibrium. And this equilibrium is reached only when a quantity called *entropy* (see Box 3.2) of the system is a maximum. So one must first maximise the entropy etc., before finding $\langle E_\nu(T)\rangle$. This is briefly hinted at in Fig. 3.4, and we shall return to this point in the next chapter.

In a sense, all this is what Rayleigh had done earlier but he did not get the right answer, i.e., an answer which agreed with the experiment. Planck decided instead to work back and see what he got. He figured that somewhere in going from step (1) to step (4), a "mistake" was being made. Where was it? Why not try to trace it by starting with the correct result, i.e., (3.6) and going backwards?

Planck did just that and finally found that he must have

$$\langle E_\nu(T)\rangle = \frac{h\nu}{e^{h\nu/k_BT} - 1} \tag{3.7}$$

In turn this implies the following:

1. $\langle n_\nu(T)\rangle$ the average quantum number of an oscillator of frequency ν at temperature T is given by

$$\langle n_\nu(T)\rangle = \frac{1}{e^{h\nu/k_BT} - 1}, \tag{3.8}$$

a result we have encountered earlier.
2. An oscillator of frequency can have only the energies

$$E_\nu = nh\nu, \quad n = 0, 1, 2, 3, ... \tag{3.9}$$

Let me now add some comments. Firstly about (3.8) which implies the following: Let us say that we have a large number of oscillators, and that this collection of oscillators is maintained at a temperature T. The heat energy would then be distributed among the various oscillators in a certain optimum manner. One might instead say that by absorbing energy from the heat source, the oscillators get excited. There might be more oscillators excited with a frequency ν_1, rather few excited with some other frequency ν_2, and so on. Formula (3.8) gives us the *average* quantum number of an oscillator with a frequency ν and at the temperature T. Later I shall indicate how one goes about finding this quantity $\langle n_\nu(T)\rangle$. The correct result in (3.8) is radically different from what the classical theory gives, namely (2.4).

As for formula (3.9), what it says is that an oscillator of frequency ν can have only *discrete* energy levels, i.e., at 0, $h\nu$, $2h\nu$, $3h\nu$, . . . , etc. Prior to Planck, people thought that an oscillator could be made to have any energy whatsoever, which is another way of saying that the oscillator energy levels are *continuous*. Planck's analysis of the blackbody radiation problem showed that this was not true. Of course since the numerical value of h is very very small, the energy difference $h\nu$ between adjacent energy levels is *extremely tiny* compared to what we usually deal with, but the fact remains that the energy levels of an oscillator *are quantised.* This quantisation becomes very important in the atomic world.

Consider now the result

$$\langle E_\nu(T)\rangle = \frac{h\nu}{e^{h\nu/k_BT} - 1} \tag{3.10}$$

If $h\nu << k_BT$ (the symbol << means *much less than*), i.e., if the temperature is very high, then

$$\langle E_\nu(T)\rangle \sim k_BT \tag{3.11}$$

which is a result known from classical physics, i.e., pre-quantum physics. If one uses this result to calculate $\rho(\nu, T)$, then one ends up with Rayleigh's law (3.4). It was Planck's genius that he was able to see that one really needed (3.8) and (3.9).

As I just said, (3.11) works at high temperatures. Why is this so? Figure 3.5 attempts an explanation. At every temperature T, there is a natural energy scale k_BT which is some kind of an energy "yardstick". Oscillator levels are looked at with this yardstick. If the temperature is high, then the oscillator levels appear quite crowded. In fact they seem continuous on the scale at which one is looking, permitting a classical picture. On the other hand, at low temperatures the energy scale k_BT gets shrunk so much that the discreteness of the oscillator levels become quite important, i.e., quantum effects can no longer be ignored.

Incidentally, Planck's theory and some extensions to it made immediately thereafter are nowadays referred to as the *old quantum theory*, to distinguish it from modern quantum mechanics. Niels Bohr borrowed Planck's ideas and took them into the world of atoms. This worked for a while until Heisenberg and Schroedinger gave us a good and solid replacement; see *The Quantum Revolution*, Part I.

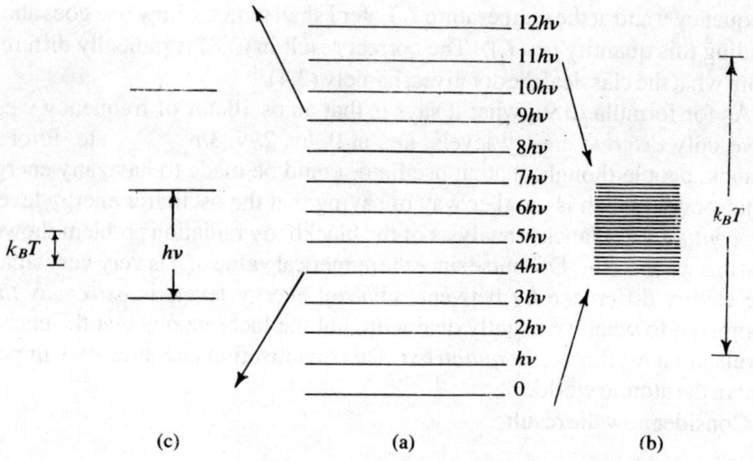

Fig. 3.5 The energy levels of an oscillator are always quantised, as shown in (a). However, depending upon the temperature T, they might *appear* to be either crowded as in (b) or sparse as in (c). This is because one always looks at the oscillator levels on a particular scale of energy (yardstick) which is decided by the temperature. The yardstick has a "length" k_BT, but since T varies, so does the length of this stick. At high temperatures the stick can encompass many oscillator levels as in (b). As a result one can take the levels to be almost continuous, which is what one does in classical physics. In short, classical physics will work at sufficiently high temperatures, despite the fact that oscillator levels are actually quantised. Obviously, it is the other way round at low temperatures where, as you can see from (c), the levels no longer appear crowded. Quantum effects therefore show up very distinctly.

3.3 Some additional comments

Section 3.2 might create the impression that Planck did some "cooking"— not really! No doubt, to start with, Planck merely guessed the correct answer, but later he did derive the formula, even though you might say in a backward direction. It is rather interesting that Planck followed a classical route and yet arrived at a correct result. How come? Basically because Planck was shrewd enough not to press classical arguments when they did not work. He knew the correct answer, i.e., (3.6) and there was no way he could get it by assuming that the oscillator was permitted a *continuous* spectrum of energy levels. A continuous energy spectrum is what classical theory demands and when Lord Rayleigh followed that line he got a wrong answer for the blackbody spectrum. Planck discovered that without (3.9) the correct blackbody spectrum could not be obtained.

In other words, Planck was *forced* to the quantisation rule. I am mentioning this merely to emphasise that Bose derived Planck's law without any of this forcing business. He quietly introduced the right assumptions at the start, and the final result came out smoothly as a logical consequence—for details you have to wait till section 3.6.

3.4 The golden year —1905

In his derivation of Planck's law, Bose made free use of Einstein's idea that light is made up of corpuscles or packets (later named the photon). It is necessary therefore to briefly refer to Einstein's pioneering idea.

The year 1905 is a remarkable milestone in the history of Physics. In this year, Albert Einstein published three monumental papers (see Box 3.3), each containing a gem of an idea and each triggering a chain of developments. Some people even say that Einstein deserved a Nobel Prize for each one of these ideas but of course he got only one. You might think it was for his discovery of the theory of relativity. In fact most people think so but that is wrong. He got it for explaining *the photoelectric effect*, which is the next part of our story.

> **Box 3.3** Volume 17 of the German physics journal the *Annalen der Physik* corresponding to the year 1905 carries three landmark papers by Einstein. On page 132 is the paper on the photoelectric effect, to which a reference is made in the text. Later, on page 549 begins the famous paper on Brownian motion, and finally on page 891 starts the paper on the special theory of relativity. This particular issue of the journal is now a collector's item.

Like everyone else, Einstein was impressed with Planck's discovery, but at the same time, he was not quite satisfied with the derivation given by Planck. And so he set about examining Planck's result in his own way. He did this in the limit considered by Wien (i.e., high frequencies), and then found that radiation behaved as if it was a *low density gas of particles*.

Einstein did not bring in material oscillators. Planck introduced the latter and from that was forced to conclude that the energy levels of a material oscillator are quantised. Einstein analysed the blackbody problem by considering radiation alone, and came to the conclusion that it was composed of quanta (see Box 3.4).

Einstein did not stop there. He used the light quantum idea to explain the phenomenon of photoelectricity (see Box 3.5). Einstein's predictions were put to strict test by several people, particularly Millikan (remembered for his accurate determination of the value of the electronic charge), and by 1915–1916 everyone was convinced that Einstein's photoelectric equation was just perfect, having explained facts which the previously

Box 3.4 Einstein introduced the light quantum hypothesis in these words:

> Monochromatic radiation of low density [i.e., within the validity of Wien's law] behaves in thermodynamic respect as if it consists of mutually independent energy quanta of magnitude $(R\beta\nu/N)$.

Today we would use the Planck's constant *h* in place of $(R\beta/N)$ for that is what the latter is. Einstein went on to say:

> If in regard to the volume dependence of the entropy, monochromatic radiation (of sufficiently low density) behaves as a discrete medium consisting of energy quanta of magnitude $(R\beta\nu/N)$, then this suggests an enquiry as to whether the laws of generation and the conversion of light are also constituted as if light were to consist of energy quanta of this kind.

Box 3.5 The photoelectric effect was discovered by Hertz in 1887. You might remember that Hertz was the person who by experiments first showed that electromagnetic waves can actually be generated in the laboratory, as predicted by Maxwell's equations. Now Hertz was fooling around with discharges (see figure (a)), and he found that a spark from one plate generated a secondary spark on the second plate. This led to a lot of careful experiments and Hertz finally concluded that the secondary sparks were really produced by light flashes near the first plate. In the following year, Wilhelm Hallwachs showed that irradiation with ultraviolet light causes uncharged metallic bodies to acquire a positive charge; it seemed as if light was causing the metal plate to lose

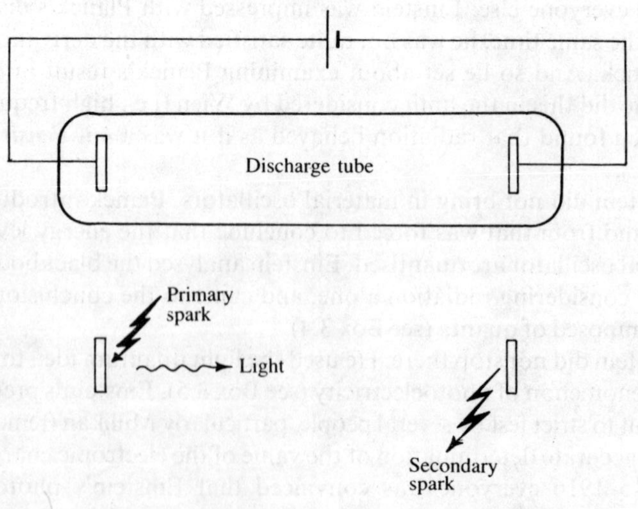

(a)

negative charge. No progress was made during the next few years, until J.J. Thomson in England discovered the electron in 1897. Three years later, Thomson was able to explain Hallwach's observations—the plate was becoming positively charged because it was emitting electrons when light fell on it. The next major discovery was by Lenard in 1902. He varied the incident light intensity by as much as a thousand times, but found that the emitted electron had the same energy. This was most puzzling as people thought that if the metal plate was illuminated with a very intense light source, then the electron should be kicked out of it with much greater energy. Einstein solved the mystery in 1905. What he said can be understood with the help of figure (b) Shown here are a number of energy levels available to the electrons in the metal. When the metal absorbs a photon of energy $h\nu$, that much of energy becomes available to the electron in making its escape.

Consider first an electron at the topmost level A. You would think that since this fellow has received an energy $h\nu$, he will have a kinetic energy $E_{\text{kin}} = h\nu$; no Sir! There is an exit tax collected by the metal when electrons leave and the technical name for it is *work function.* (When we go abroad, we have to pay such a tax; it is called foreign travel tax.) If W denotes the work function, the electron at A will have an energy

$$E_{\text{kin}} = h\nu - W \tag{1}$$

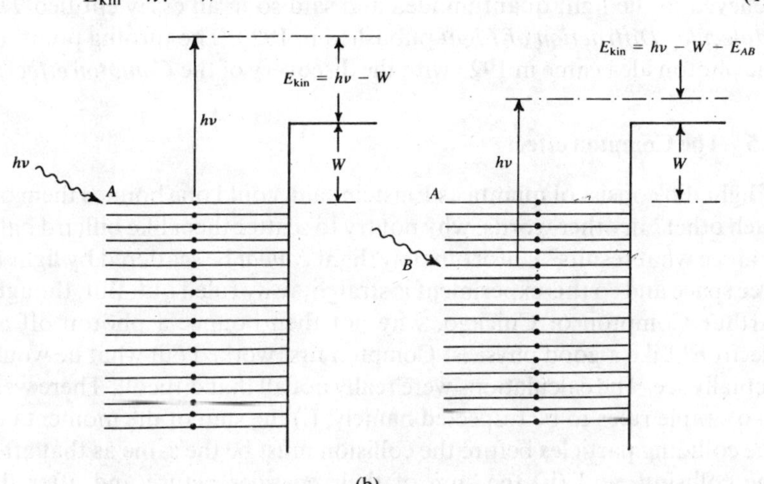

(b)

when it comes out. An electron trying to escape from a deeper level such as B has a harder task. First it would have spent an energy E_{AB} to get to the top and then pay the tax W to get out. So when it finally becomes free, its kinetic energy would be

$$E_{\text{kin}} = h\nu - E_{AB} - W \tag{2}$$

There are many more details but those do not concern us here. Robert Millikan of the U.S.—famous for his accurate measurement of the charge of the electron—did a very careful series of experiments between 1914 and 1915 and completely verified Einstein's theory of the photoelectric effect in all its aspects. He also obtained a very good value for the Planck's constant h.

successful wave theory of light could not. And it is for this that Einstein received in 1922 the Nobel Prize in Physics. But curiously, people would not believe in his idea of the light quantum. As mentioned before, the light quantum is now called the *photon*, a name given by the American chemist Gilbert Lewis in 1926. Among those who doubted Einstein were: Planck himself, the Dutch physicist Lorentz and Niels Bohr. Maxwell's theory of electromagnetic radiation was so successful that no one wanted to give it up, photoelectric effect or no photoelectric effect. At one stage, Einstein suggested an experiment which he thought would settle once and for all whether light was wave-like or corpuscular. However, Raman pointed out a flaw in Einstein's reasoning and showed that the proposed experiment would not settle the issue. Incidentally, Raman himself strongly believed in the light quantum idea and said so in an essay entitled *The Molecular Diffraction of Light* published in 1922. The turning point for the photon idea came in 1923 with the discovery of the *Compton effect*.

3.5 The Compton effect

If light did consist of quanta as Einstein said, could one bounce them off each other? In other words, why not try to scatter them like billiard balls and see what results? Unfortunately, light *cannot* be scattered by light in free space and so this experiment is straightaway ruled out. But, thought Arthur Compton of Chicago, why not then bounce a photon off an electron? Like a good physicist Compton first worked out what he would actually see. The calculations were really not all that difficult. There were two simple rules to be respected namely, (i) the sum of the momenta of the colliding particles before the collision must be the same as that after the collision, and (ii) the sum of their energies before and after the collision would also remain unchanged. In slightly more formal language, the scattering event must *conserve* both momentum and energy.

And so Compton supposed that a photon of momentum $\hbar\mathbf{k}$ (corresponding to a frequency ν and wavelength λ) collided with an electron and that after the collision the photon acquired a new momentum $\hbar\mathbf{k}'$ (corresponding to a frequency ν' and wavelength λ'). Here $\mathbf{k}$ is the wave vector, $|\mathbf{k}|$ being equal to $(2\pi/\lambda)$.

Having received a powerful kick and absorbed some energy from the incident photon, (see Fig. 3.6), the electron too would change its energy and momentum. Since the incident photon has given some of its energy to the electron, the scattered photon would naturally have a lesser energy than the incident photon. In turn this would mean that the scattered photon would have a lower frequency or, what amounts to the same thing, a longer wavelength (i.e., $\lambda' > \lambda$). Compton showed that the wavelength change $\Delta\lambda$ is given by

$$\Delta\lambda = \lambda' - \lambda = \frac{h}{m_e c}(1 - \cos\theta) \tag{3.12}$$

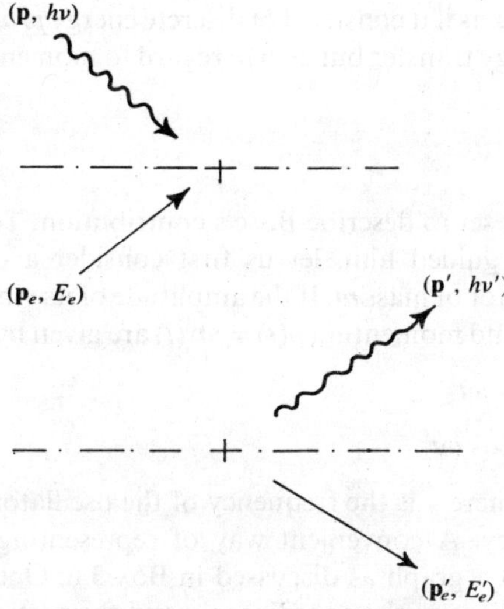

Fig. 3.6 The Compton effect essentially describes the collision of a photon with an electron as a result of which the electron receives a kick and the photon loses energy. (a) shows a photon of energy $h\nu$ and momentum $\mathbf{p}$ ($|\mathbf{p}| = h\nu/c$) about to make a collision with an electron with energy E_e and momentum $\mathbf{p}_e$. After the collision, the electron goes away with a kinetic energy E_e' and momentum $\mathbf{p}_e'$. The photon also gets deflected, besides losing energy of course. The scattering of the photon by the electron is naturally governed by the rules of conservation of energy and of momentum, i.e.,

$$E_e + h\nu = E_e' + h\nu'$$
$$\mathbf{p}_e + \mathbf{p} = \mathbf{p}_e' + \mathbf{p}'.$$

Using these rules, Compton calculated the change in the wavelength of the photon upon scattering and obtained the formula (3.12). He then performed an experiment to verify his formula.

where m_e is the mass of the electron and θ is the angle between the directions of the incident and the scattered radiation. By careful experiments using X-ray photons, Compton demonstrated that the above formula is indeed obeyed. As he wrote in his paper, "The experimental support of the theory [proposed by him and leading to eqn (3.12)] indicates very convincingly that a radiation quantum carries with it directed momentum as well as energy." In other words, the light quantum was a reality.

Compton's discovery created a sensation, and overnight the resistance to the photon idea evaporated. People now began to slowly realise that radiation had a dual character. In other words, apart from the already familiar wave-like character, radiation also had a particle-like one. As Einstein himself wrote, "Compton's experiment proves that radiation behaves as if it consisted of discrete energy *projectiles*, not only in regard to energy transfer but also in regard to momentum transfer."

3.6 Enter Bose

The stage is now set to describe Bose's contribution. To appreciate the thoughts which guided him, let us first consider a one-dimensional harmonic oscillator of mass m. If the amplitude of its vibration is A, then its position $x(t)$ and momentum $p(t) = mv(t)$ are given by

$$x(t) = A \sin \omega t$$

$$p(t) = mA \cos \omega t$$

Here $\omega = 2\pi\nu$ where ν is the frequency of the oscillator; ω is called the *angular* frequency. A convenient way of representing this behaviour would be to plot a graph as discussed in Box 3.6. One takes the horizontal axis to represent the coordinate x and the vertical axis to represent the momentum p. This two-dimensional space is said to be the *phase space* for the oscillator. Suppose the oscillator energy is E corresponding to the amplitude A. If now we consider the values of x and of p at various times 0, t_1, t_2, t_3, . . . etc., i.e., if we consider the pairs of numbers [$x(0)$, $p(0)$], [$x(t_1)$, $p(t_1)$], [$x(t_2)$, $p(t_2)$], . . . etc., and plot them, we would obtain an ellipse as discussed in Box 3.6. As the particle oscillates, so do $x(t)$ and $p(t)$. Correspondingly, the point [$x(t)$, $p(t)$] representing the *state of the oscillator at time t* moves on the ellipse which is called the *phase-space trajectory* of the oscillator. The size of the ellipse depends on the oscillator energy.

A classical oscillator can have any energy and correspondingly ellipses of all sizes are possible. For a quantum oscillator the situation is different. Planck's work revealed that only certain trajectories are allowed (see

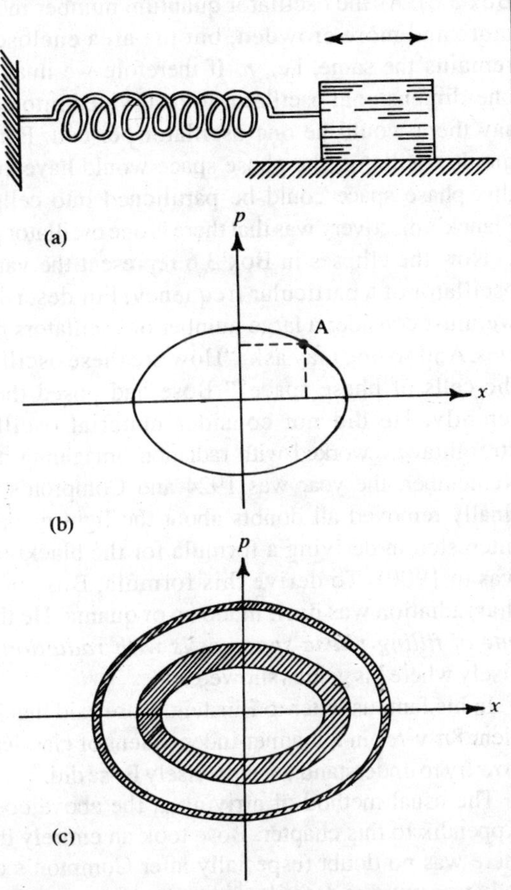

Box 3.6 This box is intended to explain what is meant by phase space and trajectories in that space. When we usually talk of space, we mean the space we live in. However, mathematicians and physicists deal with all kinds of spaces; phase space is one such. Consider the oscillator in (a). It moves in one dimension and therefore its physical space is one-dimensional. Now as the oscillator is moving back and forth, its velocity is constantly changing in magnitude and occasionally also in sign. Suppose I want to keep track of all this information, i.e., the positions and the velocities (or momentum; remember, momentum = mass × velocity). Phase space offers a convenient means of doing this. Let us denote the position of our oscillator at time t by $x(t)$ and its momentum at the same instant by $p(t)$. I now mark an x-axis and a p-axis as shown in (b), and plot a point A with coordinates $[x(t), p(t)]$. The two-dimensional space spanned by these two axes is the phase space of our (one-dimensional) oscillator. The point A represents the state of the oscillator at the time t. As the oscillator keeps oscillating and changing its state, this point also moves correspondingly in phase space tracing a trajectory. For a harmonic oscillator, the phase-space trajectory is an ellipse. Since a classical oscillator can assume any energy, all kinds of ellipses are possible. Not so for a quantum oscillator, like the one first introduced by Planck. Since only specific energy states are allowed, correspondingly only the associated ellipses are allowed. The area between adjacent ellipses is always equal to h, the Planck's constant. Of course, when the oscillator energy becomes high (i.e., the integer n in the formula $E_\nu = nh\nu$ becomes very large), the spacing between adjacent ellipses becomes very small, as illustrated in (c). Thus, when n is very much larger than unity ($n >> 1$), the quantum oscillator behaves like the classical one.

Box 3.6). As the oscillator quantum number increases, the ellipses appear more and more crowded, but the area enclosed between adjacent ones remains the same, i.e., h. If therefore we imagine the phase space of our one-dimensional oscillator to be divided into cells each of area h, we can say there would be one oscillator per cell. For a three-dimensional harmonic oscillator, the phase space would have six dimensions. Once again this phase space could be partitioned into cells, this time of volume h^3. Planck's discovery was that there is one oscillator per cell of volume h^3.

Now the ellipses in Box 3.6 represent the various possible states for an oscillator of a particular frequency. For describing blackbody radiation, we must consider a large number of oscillators having all sorts of frequencies. And so one may ask: "How are these oscillators distributed amongst the cells of phase space?" Bose had posed the question somewhat differently. He did not consider material oscillators at all. Instead, he straightaway worked with radiation, imagining it to be made up of quanta. Remember, the year was 1924 and Compton's sensational discovery had finally removed all doubts about the light quantum. To repeat, Bose was interested in deriving a formula for the blackbody spectrum (like Planck was in 1900). To derive this formula, Bose began with Einstein's idea that radiation was itself made up of quanta. He then *viewed the problem as one of filling phase-space cells with radiation quanta.* And this is precisely where his genius showed up.

In his famous letter to Einstein, Bose said that he had deduced the coefficient $8\pi \nu^2/c^3$ in a manner independent of classical electrodynamics. Let us now try to understand what precisely Bose did.

The usual method of arriving at the above coefficient is outlined in the Appendix to this chapter. Bose took an entirely different route. In his mind there was no doubt (especially after Compton's decisive experiments) that radiation must be described in terms of quanta of energy or photons (see Box 3.7). Now a photon possesses a momentum. Therefore, it can conveniently be regarded as a particle. If **p** denotes the momentum, then the components satisfy the equality

$$p_x^2 + p_y^2 + p_z^2 = p^2 = (h\nu/c)^2$$

Notice that $(p_x^2 + p_y^2 + p_z^2 = p^2)$ is the equation of the surface of a sphere of radius p. We can similarly visualise a neighbouring sphere of radius $(p+dp) = (h/c)(\nu+d\nu)$. Therefore, the volume between these two spheres is given by

$$\frac{4\pi h^2 \nu^2}{c^2} \cdot \frac{h d\nu}{c}$$

If V is the volume of the radiation cavity, the associated phase space volume is

$$V = \frac{4\pi \nu^2 \, d\nu \, h^3}{c^3}.$$

Since radiation can have two states of (linear) polarisation (perpendicular to each other), Bose multiplied the above result by 2 to obtain

A = no. of phase-space cells available for occupation

$$= \frac{8\pi \nu^2 \, d\nu \, h^3 V}{c^3} \div h^3 \qquad \text{(since each cell has a volume } h^3\text{)}$$

$$= \frac{8\pi \nu^2 \, d\nu \, V}{c^3} \tag{3.13}$$

I would like you to appreciate that result (3.13) has been obtained strictly by regarding radiation in terms of photons instead of waves, as used to be done previously (see Appendix). Though Bose did this in a bland and matter-of-fact way, it was a bold and radical departure with far-reaching consequences.

Now, blackbody radiation covers an entire spectrum. Let us focus on two adjacent frequencies ν_s and $\nu_s + d\nu_s$. Using (3.13), we can then write down an expression for A_s the number of phase-space cells. Now some of these cells may be empty, some may have just one photon of frequency ν_s, some may have two photons of the same frequency, some may have three photons, and so on (see Box 3.7). Let p_{s0} be the number of cells containing 0 photons, p_{s1} the number of cells containing 1 photon, p_{s2} the number of cells containing 2 photons, etc. The total number N_s of photons in the narrow frequency interval between ν_s and $\nu_s + d\nu_s$ is therefore given by

Box 3.7 It may be a good idea to paraphrase here what a *photon* means. It is a "quantum" of the electromagnetic field with the following properties:

1. It has a definite frequency ν and a definite wave vector $\mathbf{k}$.
2. The wave vector is a vector, the direction of which indicates the direction of propagation of the photon.
3. The magnitude of the wave vector is given by

   $$|\mathbf{k}| = k = 2\pi/\lambda,$$

   where $\lambda = c/\nu$, is the wavelength and c is the velocity of light/photon.
4. The energy E of the photon is given by $E = h\nu$.
5. The photon has a momentum $\mathbf{p} = \hbar\mathbf{k}$ note that $\mathbf{p} = (h\nu/c)$.
6. The mass of the photon is zero; observe that even though the mass is zero, the photon still has a momentum.
7. The photon also has a spin angular momentum, about which more will be said in Chapter 5.

$$N_s = 0 \cdot p_{s0} + 1 \cdot p_{s1} + 2 \cdot p_{s2} + \ldots \tag{3.14}$$

Bose now said that the number of different ways in which these photons can be arranged amongst the A_s cells is

$$\frac{A_s!}{p_{s0}!\, p_{s1}!\, p_{s2}! \ \ldots} \tag{3.15}$$

Here, I have introduced a new notation. If n is an integer, then $n!$ (read n factorial) is defined as

$$1 \cdot 2 \cdot 3 \cdot \ldots \cdot (n-1) \cdot n \tag{3.16}$$

With this notation, the meaning of (3.15) should be clear.

Now in writing (3.15), Bose assumed that the photons are indistinguishable. In Chapter 4, I shall have more comments on this formula.

So far, we have considered the number of different arrangements for photons of just one frequency ν_s. Since all frequencies are present in the radiation cavity, we have to multiply formulae like (3.15) for each one of these frequencies. Thus the total number of possible arrangements is given by

$$W = \prod_s \left\{ \frac{A_s!}{p_{s0}!\, p_{s1}!\, p_{s2}! \ \ldots} \right\} \tag{3.17}$$

where the symbol Π means continued multiplication or continued product just as Σ means summation. The energy E available for distribution is fixed and so we obviously must have it equal to the sum of the energies of all the photons present, i.e.,

$$E = \sum_s N_s \cdot h\nu_s \tag{3.18}$$

where

$$N_s = \sum_r r p_{sr}, \quad r = 0, 1, 2, \ldots \tag{3.19}$$

There are a few more steps involved and they relate essentially to the maximisation of the entropy (see Fig.3.4).

Let us pause and absorb what has been said so far. The problem is to derive an expression for the radiation energy density in the frequency interval between ν and $\nu + d\nu$. Planck did this by starting with material oscillators which transferred their energy to standing waves in the cavity. In his analysis of Planck's work, Einstein supposed that radiation behaved like a gas of particles, and so he distributed the available energy E amongst these gas particles. Now Bose is trying to do the same thing, although he doesn't talk of gas particles; but he is considering particles all the same for photons can be regarded as such. So, where is the difference? In many places really. First of all, unlike Einstein, Bose does not regard his particles as distinguishable. Einstein did not make a big fuss about his particles being distinguishable or anything like that. In those days, nobody ever considered indistinguishable particles, and like everybody else, Einstein simply assumed (implicitly) that his particles were distinguishable. How come then, that he obtained a correct result with an incorrect assumption? That is because to get at the final answer Einstein appealed to Wien's law which, you remember, works at high frequencies. In other words, Einstein got away because he forced agreement with experimental data (at high frequencies). Today we would employ fancier language and say, in a manner of speaking, that Einstein used the *correspondence principle* (see Box 3.8).

What about Bose? Without even bothering to declare it, he treats photons to be indistinguishable. True he did not say so explicitly in words but the formula he used for counting the number of possible arrangements meant *precisely* that. To him, this was the most natural thing to do. Only later did people realise that Bose had taken a remarkable step which he did not even care to explain in any detail. This was not all; the photon can have two states of polarization, and Bose took that also in his stride. Today we would say that Bose took proper care of photon spin (more about this in Chapter 5). And lastly, he tacitly assumed that photon number is not conserved.

Seldom has a person taken so many bold steps all at one time, almost unconsciously. Was it logic that was compelling him or the hands of destiny? I do not know. Anyway, Bose did all that I described above. Years later he said,

> I had no idea that what I had done was really novel... I was not a statistician to the extent of really knowing that I was doing something which was really different from what Boltzmann would have done...

OK, so Bose started off in a novel way. The rest was easy for there was now a standard path. I shall not describe it here, reserving it for Chapter 4. In any case the end result was not anything new—it was the old Planck formula again. What was dramatically different was the *starting point* of Bose. Let me therefore add some more comments on that.

We must remember the year was 1924. Quantum mechanics was just about to make its entry. The photon had just been accepted. People did not know anything about spin, about Bosons and Fermions, and that they obeyed different statistics, etc. All these developments occurred rapidly within the next few years. Many people made discoveries and every discovery influenced every other. It is against this background we must see Bose's contribution to appreciate how it merged into the mainstream to contribute to the pool of knowledge.

Bose achieved two things *ahead* of quantum mechanics. First, *he discovered*

Box 3.8 I have already pointed out that the quantum revolution started with the discovery by Planck that the energy levels of a harmonic oscillator are restricted to the values $E = nh\nu$, where n is an integer and ν the frequency of the oscillator. Energy transfers *to* and *from* the oscillator take place in quanta with energy equal to $h\nu$—I mean the oscillator could emit one or more quanta, or absorb one or more of these, depending on the circumstances. These quanta are indivisible. Later in 1913, Bohr applied the quantum idea to the atom. Till proper quantum mechanics was developed, these ideas of Planck and of Bohr provided the general guidelines for those exploring the world of atoms.

In those days, Bohr had a simple advice for the explorer. He said in effect,"If you find anything new, make sure that when many quanta are involved, you get a result which agrees with the predictions of classical mechanics." This is another way of saying (essentially) that in the limit of large quantum numbers, quantum results tend to classical ones. This advice of Bohr is formally referred to as the *Bohr correspondence principle*. Bohr made good use of this principle. Whenever he deduced something new using quantum ideas he would check to see what result he got in the limit of large quantum numbers. That result agreed with an already known and well established result, his guess work was OK. H.A.Kramers, who made important contributions to quantum mechanics writes,

> It is difficult to explain what the correspondence principle consists of, because it cannot be expressed in exact quantitative terms, and it is, on this account, also difficult to apply. In Bohr's hands it has been extraordinarily fruitful in the most varied fields.

indistinguishability. As I shall point out in Chapter 5, indistinguishability is a natural product of quantum mechanics having its roots in the famous Heisenberg uncertainty principle. But Bose *sensed* indistinguishability even earlier. Secondly, after people realised that quantum mechanics *demands* indistinguishability, they also found that there were two broad families of indistinguishable particles namely, Bosons and Fermions. It was discovered that even though Bosons (of a given type or species) may be indistinguishable, things happen when one tries to swap them; same with Fermions. The effects of swapping are described in terms of wave functions (as I shall explain in Chapter 5). In the end, what all this means is that when there are identical Bosons or Fermions and one wants to distribute some energy amongst them, then one has to have rules like (2.1), (2.2) and (2.3). In other words, after quantum mechanics came quantum statistical mechanics, which essentially deals with how quantum particles share energy at finite temperatures. By contrast, in the quantum mechanics as developed by Heisenberg and Schroedinger, there is no temperature. So, quantum statistical mechanics was the next step on the new road. *Bose laid part of the foundation for quantum statistical mechanics even before quantum mechanics was born!*

Now you know why people are amazed that so much had been packed so innocently into one, "ordinary-looking", four-page paper.

Much ground has been covered in this chapter. Since I have criss-crossed quite a bit, you might even be confused. A summary is therefore essential.

To sum up:

- Bose's contribution was made during an eventful period in the history of physics.
- It came immediately after Compton's discovery confirming the light quantum but before Heisenberg and Schroedinger ushered in quantum mechanics.
- Bose was simply trying to rederive Planck's law but in a manner free from logical loopholes.
- Planck derived his law by starting with material oscillators in the walls of the cavity. The oscillators transferred their energy to electromagnetic waves of the corresponding frequency. Planck found that the oscillator energy levels are given by (3.9) and their average number at a temperature T by (3.8).
- At high temperatures, the classical result is recovered—see (3.11).
- In 1905 Einstein examined Planck's law carefully. He did not start with the material oscillators of Planck. Instead, he supposed that radiation is like a gas of particles. Einstein treated the gas like a *classical gas*, but he could get away with it because he made sure that his analysis was in accord with Wien's law at high frequencies. Today we would say that Einstein used Bohr's correspondence principle. The final outcome of Einstein's analysis was that radiation behaved like it was made up of quanta with energy $h\nu$.
- Although Einstein considered a *photon gas* he did not bring in indistinguishability. He did not even know about it. Nor did he bother about whether the number of photons was conserved or not. In fact, he had *no* need to, because he was forcing the correct answer anyway.
- Like Einstein, Bose also considered a photon gas. Therefore, he too dealt with radiation quanta. But he did not force any agreement with experiment. He simply decided to distribute these quanta into cells in phase space. In so doing, he remembered Planck's discovery—there must be one oscillator per cell of volume h^3 in phase space. Using this result, he was able to figure out how many cells are available for radiation, between frequency ν_s and $\nu_s + d\nu_s$, to occupy.
- Having found the accommodation available, Bose distributed his pho-

tons into these cells. Quite naturally, he made the distribution treating the photons as

1. indistinguishable
2. if their number was not conserved
3. if they had spin 1

- All three are remarkable steps—but hardly any comments about them were made by Bose in his epoch-making paper.
- Starting with these remarkable steps, Bose derived Planck's law for the first time in a clean and logical manner. He then wrote up his results and sent the manuscript to Einstein.
- When Einstein received Bose's manuscript, in a flash he saw the significance of these radical steps and built upon them. That story appears in Chapter 7.

In the next few chapters, I shall catch up with all the things I had promised to explain.

Appendix to Chapter 3

Normal modes of radiation in a cavity

The idea of normal modes is best understood by considering first a vibrating string. Let the string be stretched and clamped at the ends as in figure a(i). The string can vibrate in different ways as in a(ii), a(iii), etc. The patterns as in a(ii), a(iii), etc., are called the *normal modes* of the vibrating string. Each mode is a characteristic vibrational pattern. When the string is plucked in an arbitrary manner, there is a complex superposition of the various possible normal modes. Observe that the normal modes differ in the number of wavelengths they accommodate over the length L of the string. The more the ripples, the shorter is the wavelength. Related to the wavelength λ is the wave vector k, defined by $k = 2\pi/\lambda$. There is of course also the vibrational frequency ν, and the pair of numbers (k, ν) characterise the normal mode. If we draw a horizontal line and mark all the allowed values of k, they would form a grid as shown at the bottom of figure (a).

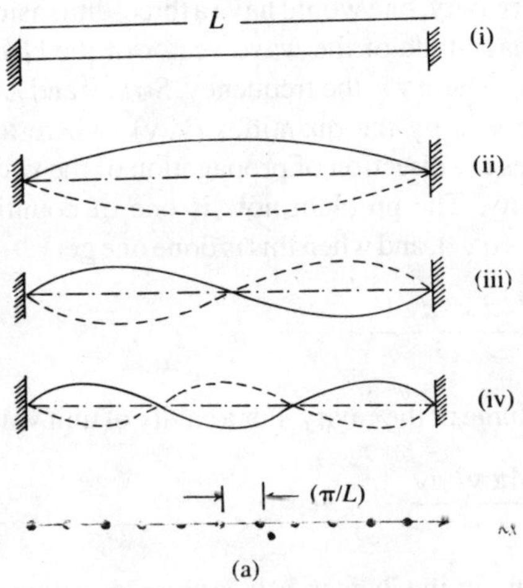

(a)

Blackbody radiation is made up of electromagnetic waves of all sorts of frequencies, and our interest, if you remember, is in the number of modes between ν and $\nu + d\nu$. In reality, the answer would depend upon the shape of the cavity but if the cavity is sufficiently big (i.e., tens of thousands of times the average wavelength, which is usually the case), then no great harm is done by assuming the cavity to have a convenient shape. Accordingly, we choose a cubical shape. We now ask what sort of waves a cubical cavity can support, and this is where the string analogy proves useful. To make this more obvious, consider a square cavity. We wish to study normal modes of this cavity which is another way of asking: "What sort of waves can this support?" The problem is

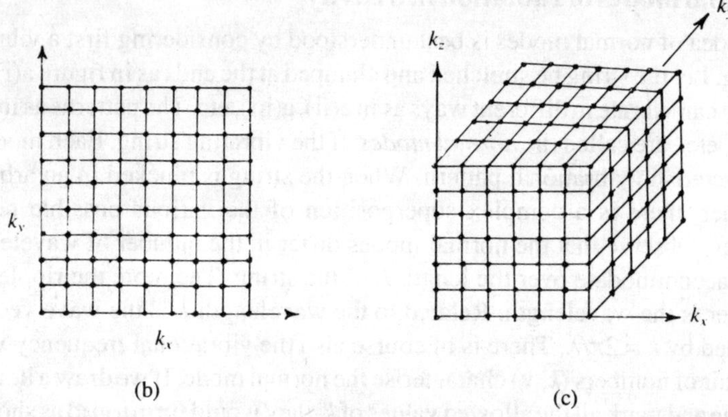

(b) (c)

the two-dimensional extension of the string problem and to cut a long story short, the allowed k values now form a lattice or a grid as in figure (b). Naturally, for a cubical cavity, one would have a three-dimensional grid as in (c).

Let k be the magnitude of the wave vector of the electromagnetic wave; $k = 2\pi/\lambda = 2\pi\nu/c$, where ν is the frequency. So k, ν and λ are all related. Each wave is characterised by the quantities ($\mathbf{k}$, ν) (where $\mathbf{k}$ is a vector whose direction indicates the direction of propagation of the wave), and is a normal mode of the cavity. The problem now is one of counting all such modes between ν and ($\nu + d\nu$), and when this is done one gets

$$G(\nu)d\nu = \frac{4\pi\nu^2 d\nu V}{c^3} \quad (1)$$

where V is the volume of the cavity. For a cavity of unit volume, the result is

$$g(\nu)d\nu = \frac{4\pi\nu^2 d\nu}{c^2} \quad (2)$$

As I shall point out in Chapter 5, in a given direction, one can have light waves of two different polarizations. So essentially, the number in (2) has to be doubled, which then gives

$$g(\nu)d\nu = \frac{8\pi\nu^2 d\nu}{c^2} \quad (3)$$

A few words finally about the relationship between the "mechanical" oscillators of Planck (assumed to be distributed on the walls of cavity) and the normal modes we are now discussing. The oscillator is the source of energy, which it pumps into the waves. Clearly, an oscillator of frequency ν can transfer energy only to a normal mode of the same frequency ν. Oscillators can lose energy to the normal mode as well as absorb energy from the normal mode—see figure (d). In the former case the energy content of the electromagnetic wave increases while in the latter case the energy content decreases. As described in section 3.4, in 1905, Einstein proposed that light energy itself is quantised. Today we refer to these light quanta as photons. So, if an oscillator of frequency ν comes down two steps in its energy, then it means that two light quanta, each of energy $h\nu$, are emitted into the cavity—this is the way we would describe things today. In fact, we would go one step further and say that it is not oscillators but atoms in the walls of the cavity which emit and absorb radiation. Einstein was the first one to connect atoms with blackbody radiation. He did that work around 1916. I describe it in Chapter 6.

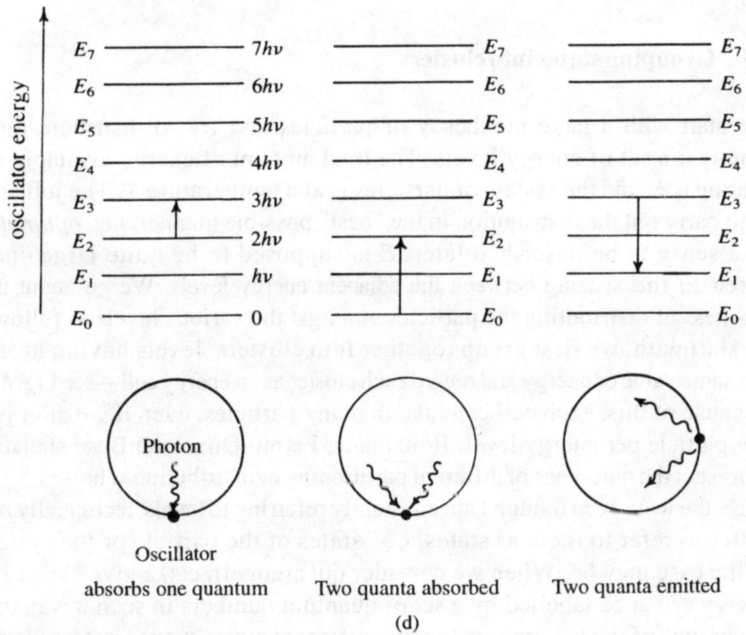

(d)

4 *Hindsight*

In the last chapter I described in historical sequence the various events culminating in the discovery made by Bose. Looking back, we can consider the problem of statistical distribution in a systematic manner as I shall describe below. This would automatically lead to rules (2.1)–(2.3) introduced earlier.

4.1 Grouping states into clusters

We start with a large number N of particles and try to distribute them amongst a set of energy levels. The total amount of energy available for sharing is E, and the system of particles is at a temperature T. The job now is to carry out the distribution in the "best" possible manner, i.e., *optimally*, in a sense to be described later. E is supposed to be quite large compared to the spacing between the adjacent energy levels. We go about this business of distributing the particles amongst the various levels as follows: To start with, we first group together into clusters, levels having nearly the same value of energy and regard each cluster as an energy cell—see Fig. 4.1. Because of this, each cell can take in many particles, even if we allot just one particle per energy level. Boltzmann, Fermi–Dirac and Bose statistics represent the outcomes of different partitioning or distribution schemes.

By the way, even though I am constantly referring to levels, technically it is better to refer to them as states, i.e., states of the particle or the system as the case may be. When we consider quantum effects, a given state j of energy ε_j can be labelled by a set of quantum numbers in such a way that the values of these numbers for two different states would not be identical. But it could happen that two states with different sets of quantum numbers have the same energy. In that case, we say that the two states are *degenerate*.

Before considering the different distribution schemes, let us agree on some notation. Let energy cell i contain g_i energy states and let n_i be the number of

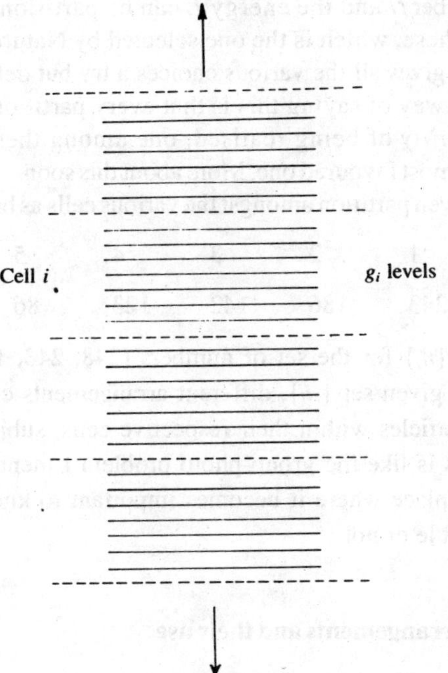

Fig. 4.1 We have here the energy levels available to a particle. There are actually N particles, and the question is: How are these to be distributed amongst the available levels? Various possibilities exist, as discussed in this chapter. For carrying out this distribution, we first group into a cluster or cell, levels having very nearly the same value for the energy. There are many such cells piled one on top of the other. Cell i has g_i levels grouped together. For convenience we assume that all the g_i levels in cell i have the same energy ε_i.

particles in this cell ($g_i > n_i$). The energy states being close, each state in this cell can be supposed to correspond to an average energy ε_i so that the total energy content of this cell is $n_i\,\varepsilon_i$. Remembering what E and N represent, we obviously have

$$N = \sum_i n_i \tag{4.1a}$$

$$E = \sum_i n_i\,\varepsilon_i \tag{4.1b}$$

The sum over i in the above equations ranges over all the occupied cells. These equations represent *constraints*, i.e., no matter how the distribution is made, these conditions *must always* be obeyed.

Now the number N and the energy E can be partitioned in many different ways. Of these, which is the one selected by Nature? It turns out that Nature actually gives all the various choices a try but definitely has preferences. A better way of saying this is that every partitioning scheme has a certain *probability* of being realised, one among these being the *most probable* or the most favoured one. More about this soon.

Consider a given partition amongst the various cells as below:

i	0	1	2	3	4	5	6	...
n_i	248	243	186	142	123	86	55	...

We shall write $\{n_i\}$ for the set of numbers (248, 243, 186, 142, 123, 86, 55, . . .). For a given set $\{n_i\}$, different arrangements can be obtained by shuffling the particles within their respective cells, subject to the rules of the game —this is like the group-photo problem I mentioned earlier. And this is also the place where it becomes important to know if the particles are distinguishable or not.

4.2 Distinct arrangements and their use

Let $W\{ni\}$ denote the number of distinct arrangements possible for a given set $\{n_i\}$ and for a given set of rules regarding the filling business. As we shall presently see, the precise formula for W depends on whether we wish to follow Bose or Fermi or Boltzmann.

OK, so there are these various formulae. What does Nature do with them? Remember what Nature's problem is. She has a total energy E and she has to distribute this amongst N particles in all. Nature now says, "I will distribute this energy in such a manner that the *entropy* is a maximum." So, to arrive at the answer we have to go through the following steps:

1. Decide first whose filling rule is to be followed, i.e., is it Bose or Fermi or Boltzmann?
2. Write down the corresponding formula for $W\{n_i\}$ (recall (3.17)).
3. Find the set $\{n_i\}$ which makes W a maximum. This is done by using what is called the *variational technique*— see Box 4.1.
4. In practice, it is more convenient to maximise the logarithm of W rather than W itself. The quantity which is maximised is given by $S = k_B \ln W$ and is already known to us (recall Box 3.2).
5. Maximum S represents a condition of thermodynamic equilibrium. The members of the set $\{n_i\}$ which makes S a maximum represent

the average values of the occupation numbers. They are temperature dependent and so we write them as $\langle n_i(T) \rangle$. So now you know how these averages are obtained; it is via Boltzmann's rule for the entropy *S*.

6. Use the above result for $\langle n_i(T) \rangle$to calculate whatever is to be cal- culated concerning the system, e.g., specific heat. There are well-defined formulae in statistical physics for doing this. Our own interest is in the radiation problem, which is discussed in section 4.5.

Box 4.1 This box offers a primer on the so-called *variational principle* or *method.* Consider figure (a) in which is plotted a function $y(x)$ which has many maxima and minima, often collectively referred to as *extrema*. If we draw a tangent to the curve at the extrema, we will find that it is horizontal, i.e.,the slope is zero. Methods exist for finding the extrema but I shall not go into that; perhaps you already know about it.

The *calculus of variations* deals with a similar but somewhat more complicated problem. Consider figure (b) where two points A and B are shown. We now draw a curve joining A and B and then spin it around the *z*-axis to generate a surface. Obviously, various surfaces can be generated by drawing various curves between A and B, and the question is: Which of these has the least area? This is the sort of problem variational calculus can tackle.

Mechanics is a subject where extensive use is made of the variational method. As you know, Newton is the father of mechanics but others who came later developed the subject further. Prominent among those who did so was Hamilton, and his great idea is now often referred to as *Hamilton's principle*. Say a bullet is fired from a point (x_1, y_1) at time t_1 and that it flies to point (x_2, y_2), reaching it at time t_2. What is the trajectory traced by the bullet? According to Hamilton's principle, the path would be one which would make the integral

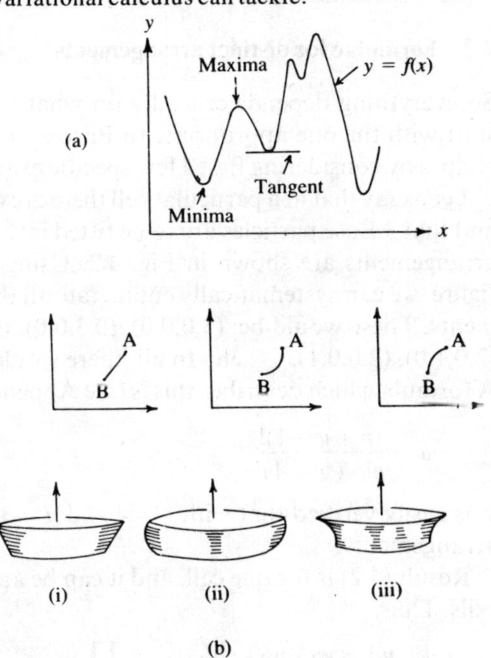

$$\int_{t_1}^{t_2} (T - V)dt$$

a minimum, where T is the kinetic energy and V the potential energy of the bullet. Maybe all this appears a bit too technical but the essential point is that to make actual use of Hamilton's principle, one must resort to the variational method. If you pursue physics, then you must not miss the famous Feynman lectures. In Vol. 2, Chapter 19 of that series, Feynman says:

> When I was in high school, my physics teacher called me down one day after physics class and said, "You look bored; I want to tell you something interesting". Then he told me something which I found absolutely fascinating, and have, since then, always found fascinating.

Feynman is referring to the *principle of least action*, the "action" being measured by the integral written above.

What have variational methods to do with the derivation of Planck's law? Well, remember that Planck was trying to distribute his oscillators amongst available states (Bose was similarly trying to distribute light quanta amongst the states). This distribution had to be done in such a manner that the entropy was a maximum (i.e., an extremum). And that precisely is where all the technology of variational calculus comes into the picture.

4.3 Formulae for distinct arrangements

So everything depends crucially on what recipe we use for W. Let us start with the one appropriate to Bosons. I shall introduce the various recipes by considering first a few specific examples.

Let us say that in a particular cell there are 4 states (which means $g = 4$), and that 3 Bose particles are to be fitted into these. Some of the possible arrangements are shown in Fig. 4.2. Using the notation shown in the figure, we can systematically enumerate all the possible distinct arrangements. These would be: (3,0,0,0), (0,3,0,0), (0,0,3,0), (0,0,0,3), (2,1,0,0), (2,0,1,0), (2,0,0,1), . . . etc. In all, there would be 20 such arrangements. A formula which describes this is (see Appendix to this chapter):

$$w = \frac{(n + g - 1)!}{n! \cdot (g - 1)!} \tag{4.2}$$

It is easily verified that with $g = 4$ and $n = 3$, the formula (4.2) gives 20 arrangements.

Result (4.2) is for one cell, and it can be applied successively to all the cells. Thus,

$$W\{n_i\} = w_1 \cdot w_2 \cdot w_3 \cdot \;. . . = \prod_i w_i$$

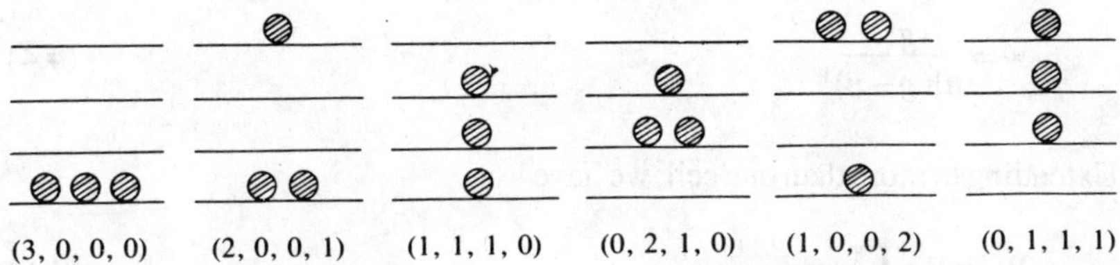

Fig. 4.2 This figure illustrates how particles are distributed when they obey Bose statistics. For convenience, only *one* cell of Fig. 4.1 is considered, and it has four levels or states clustered together, i.e., $g = 4$. True their energies have earlier been assumed to be the same but for convenience we depict the levels separated. Even though the energies of the states are the same, we must remember they carry different quantum labels and are therefore distinct. Thus we must worry about how the particles can distribute themselves amongst these levels. We suppose that there are three Bose particles, in which case there are 20 arrangements possible. Some of these are shown here.

$$= \prod_i \frac{(g_i + n_i - 1)!}{n_i!\,(g_i - 1)!} \tag{4.3}$$

This is the desired formula for the Bose case. You might observe that formula (4.3) is not the same as (3.15) written down by Bose. Actually both lead to the same result. The version in (4.3) was used by Einstein when he wrote the sequel to Bose's paper, and is the one more commonly used. I shall refer again to this sequel paper of Einstein in Chapter 7.

We now go through a similar routine for the Fermion case. Here I choose $g = 5$ and $n = 3$. As before, the particles are indistinguishable, but now, not more than one particle is allowed in each level. Sample occupation arrangements are shown in Fig. 4.3. The distinct arrangements allowed are: (1,1,1,0,0), (1,1,0,1,0), (1,1,0,0,1), (1,0,1,1,0), (1,0,1,0,1), (1,0,0,1,1),

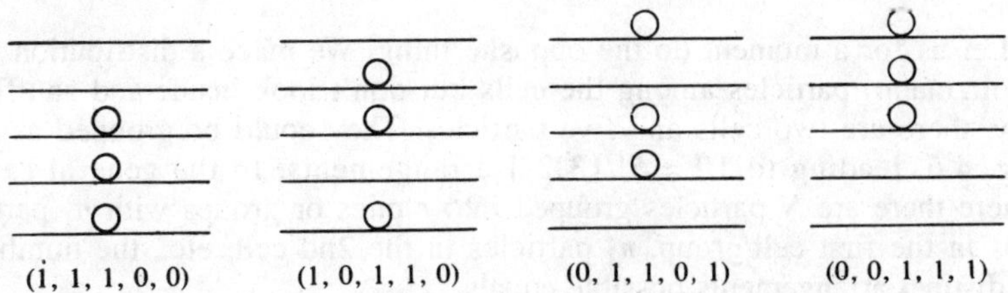

Fig. 4.3 This figure is very similar to the previous one except that here $g = 5$, and $n = 3$. Further, the particles are Fermions. Ten arrangements are possible (described in the text), of which some are shown here.

(0,1,1,1,0), (0,1,1,0,1), (0,1,0,1,1), (0,0,1,1,1). There are 10 in all, covered by the general formula

$$w = \frac{g!}{n!(g-n)!} \tag{4.4}$$

Extending to more than one cell, we have

$$\mathrm{W}\{n_i\} = \prod_i \frac{g_i!}{n_i!(g_i - n_i)!} \tag{4.5}$$

Finally the Boltzmann case. Again we start with a cell which has, this time, say, three levels amongst which two particles are distributed. The different arrangements are shown in Fig. 4.4, i.e., there are $3^2 = 9$ arrangements. In general, if there are g_i levels and n_i ($n_i < g_i$) distinguishable particles, then

$$(g_i)^{n_i} \tag{4.6}$$

arrangements can be realised in that cell alone.

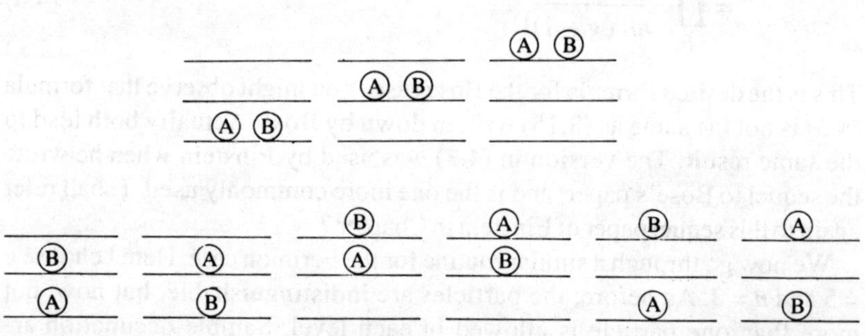

Fig. 4.4 This figure is again like the previous two, except that now $g = 3$, $n = 2$ and the particles obey Boltzmann statistics.

Let us for a moment do the opposite thing. We make a distribution of (Boltzmann) particles among the cells but don't look inside and shuffle. Say, there are two cells and five particles. They could be grouped as in Fig. 4.5, leading to $10 = 5!/\{3!2!\}$ arrangements. In the general case where there are N particles grouped into r piles or groups with n_1 particles in the first cell/group, n_2 particles in the 2nd cell, etc., the number of distinct arrangements possible equals

$$\frac{N!}{(n_1!\, n_2!\, n_3! \ldots n_r!)} \tag{4.7}$$

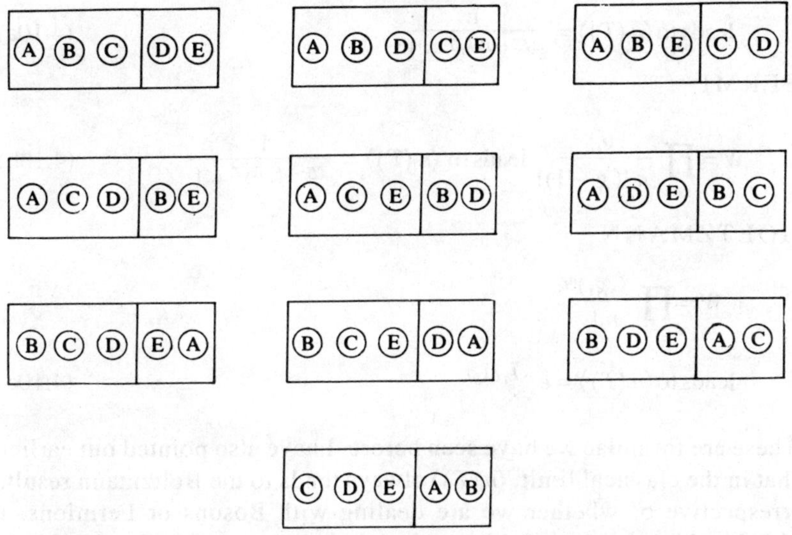

Fig. 4.5 In Fig. 4.4, we had one cell with three (degenerate) levels and we studied the different ways in which two Boltzmann particles could be distributed. We now do a slightly different exercise. We have two cells, and we agree that we will always put three particles in cell 1 and two particles in cell 2. Inside cell 1, for example, the three particles could be shuffled around amongst the g_1 available levels. This sort of thing was studied in Fig. 4.4, but here we don't worry about such internal shufflings like changing Ⓐ Ⓑ Ⓒ to Ⓐ Ⓒ Ⓑ etc. In that case, 10 arrangements are possible as shown above.

We now have to combine (4.6) and (4.7) because we not only have to distribute particles into cells but also allow for shufflings inside them. We thus get

$$W = \left[\frac{N!}{n_1!\, n_2!\, n_3! \ldots n_r!} \right] \cdot [(g_1)^{n_1} \ldots (g_r)^{n_r}]$$

$$= N! \prod_i \frac{(g_i)^{n_i}}{n_i!} \tag{4.8}$$

As mentioned in the Appendix, the factor $N!$ can be dropped, giving

$$W = \prod_i \frac{(g_i)^{n_i}}{n_i!} \tag{4.9}$$

Collecting all results together, we get:

BOSE

$$W = \prod_i \frac{(g_i + n_i - 1)!}{n_i!(g_i - 1)!}$$

$$\text{leads to} \langle n_i(T) \rangle = \frac{1}{e^{(E_i - \mu)/k_B T} - 1} \tag{4.10a}$$

FERMI

$$W = \prod_i \frac{g_i!}{n_i!(g_i - 1)!} \quad \text{leads to} \langle n_i(T) \rangle = \frac{1}{e^{(E_i - E_F)k_B T} + 1} \tag{4.10b}$$

BOLTZMANN

$$W = \prod_i \frac{(g_i)^{n_i}}{n_i!}$$

$$\text{leads to} \langle n_i(T) \rangle = e^{-E_i / k_B T} \tag{4.10c}$$

These are formulae we have seen before. I have also pointed out earlier that in the classical limit, $\langle n_i(T) \rangle$ always tends to the Boltzmann result, irrespective of whether we are dealing with Bosons or Fermions. I should add that although I have used the words "leads to" rather casually, in reality these words hide a lot of technical detail which, however, do not concern us here.

4.4 Are atoms distinguishable?

You might, if you have been thinking deeply, wonder: "In a gas like, say, argon, all the argon atoms would look alike. Where is the question of distinguishability? How do we know which atom is which? After all, they are not painted or marked." Quite true. Boltzmann had already thought about that one and had an answer. To understand his line of reasoning, let us look into the gas and see what is going on there. We would then see atoms flying all over the place at various speeds in various directions. Occasionally there would be collisions, whereupon the colliding atoms would be deflected or scattered rather like billiard balls. In classical mechanics, it is possible to follow the motion of particles via their trajectories. And so, unless the atoms come *infinitely* close to each other which of course is not possible, one can always keep track of what the different atoms are doing which is as good as giving them individual names. In a sense, this is what happens when we watch billiards and see two white balls collide. The balls are not marked but we know which ball is which *because we are able to observe their individual trajectories.* Boltzmann assumed this was possible with atoms also, which effectively made them distinguishable.

Consider what happens in the quantum case. As you probably know, precise definition of the trajectories is no longer possible; this of course is due to the famous *Heisenberg uncertainty principle* (see Box 4.2). So, when a collision between, say, two argon atoms occurs and we observe the

Box 4.2 The uncertainty principle was stated by Heisenberg soon after the first few papers, signalling the birth of quantum mechanics, had appeared. Briefly, what it says is the following: If a measurement of position of a particle is made with an accuracy Δx and if a measurement of momentum is made *simultaneously* with an accuracy Δp, then the product of the two uncertainties can never be made smaller than h (the Planck constant). In other words,

$$\Delta x \ \Delta p \sim h \qquad (1)$$

where the symbol ~ means *about* or *of the order of*.

Physicist David Bohm remarks: "The term uncertainty principle is somewhat of a misnomer. A better term would be 'the principle of limited determinism in the structure of matter'." What Bohm means is that indeterminism implied by the above equation is inherent in the very structure of matter and we talk of uncertainty because we have been brainwashed by classical physics to believe that perfect determinism is possible. According to the latter, the position and the momentum of a particle can be simultaneously measured with *infinite* precision. So what the principle of Heisenberg really means is that we the observers *cannot* measure both these quantities *simultaneously* with accuracies greater than that implied by equation (1).

About this principle, Richard Feynman has this to say:

> The uncertainty principle "protects" quantum mechanics. Heisenberg recognized that if it were possible to measure the momentum and the position simultaneously with a greater accuracy, then quantum mechanics would collapse. So he proposed that it must be impossible. Then people sat down and tried to figure out ways of doing it, and nobody could figure out a way of measuring the position and the momentum of anything—a screen, an electron, a billiard ball, anything—with any greater accuracy. Quantum mechanics maintains its perilous but still correct existence.

atoms after they have collided against each other, we can't say which of the two processes, b(ii) or b(iii) (see Fig. 4.6), has occurred. We have no means of knowing. In fact, both are possible, each with its own probability amplitude; and, when we perform scattering calculations, we must allow for both. Of course, if the particles are Bosons then the allowance is made in one way while if they are Fermions the allowance is made in a somewhat different way. The main point is that there *is* a certain amount of quantum mechanical fuzziness, which in effect contributes to indistinguishability. In the next chapter, I shall throw some more light on this.

In short, it is not as if Boltzmann imagined the atoms to be painted or anything like that. All he said was that he could *in principle* keep track of

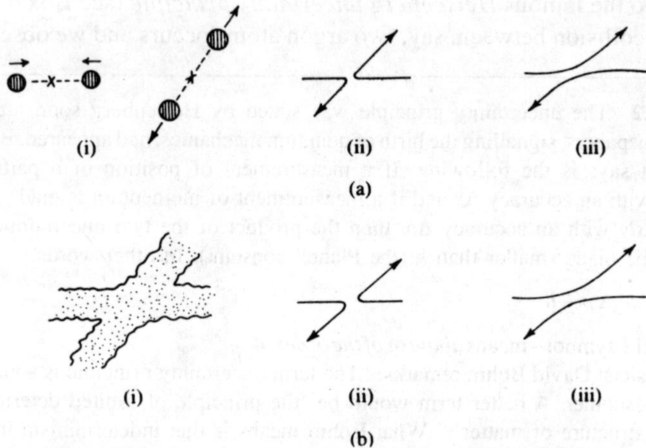

Fig. 4.6 This figure discusses with schematic diagrams the collision between two argon atoms. (a) shows the scenario in classical mechanics. It is rather like the collision of two white billiard balls. True the balls both look alike but our eyes can pick up their trajectories and so we can always say which ball went where, i.e., whether the collision occurred as in a(ii) or as in a(iii). Boltzmann assumed that this was true of atoms as well. Since individual trajectories could be clearly and precisely determined (at least in principle), the atoms were effectively *distinguishable* according to Boltzmann. Trouble arose when Heisenberg introduced his famous uncertainty principle (see Box 4.2). What now happened was that in quantum mechanics one could have only fuzzy trajectories as in b(i). You may say: "That is OK, but after the collision we should certainly be able to say which ball went where, since they are now so far apart that fuzziness should not matter any longer. In other words, we must at least be able to say that the collision occurred as per b(ii) or b(iii)." Unfortunately, in quantum mechanics this kind of argument does not work. When quantum mechanical calculations of collisions are performed we must allow for the two possibilities b(ii) and b(iii), each of which has its own probability amplitude. Sounds puzzling? See Box 5.1 for comfort!

which atom is doing what by following their trajectories, and classical mechanics (which was all that was available then), certainly permitted him to do that. By the way, using computers, one can actually study the classical collision process and trace the trajectories of the various atoms.

You might now wonder: "If quantum mechanics is the reality, then how is it that the Boltzmann formula works at high temperatures?" That is a good question. Quantum fuzziness depends on a quantity λ_{th} which I shall introduce you to in the next chapter. It is called the *thermal wavelength*. At high temperatures λ_{th} is small which also means that fuzziness is small. So it is no wonder that the use of the Boltzmann method does not lead to atrocious results at these temperatures.

Now that we are talking of hindsight, let me mention another aspect of it.

You might be puzzled why nobody had any inkling or clue about indistinguishability of particles before Bose. Was there no evidence or were there no tell-tale signs before? Yes, there were a few but nobody took serious notice. The Gibbs paradox is an example (see also, *A Hot Story*).

Remember the entropy business? One question that was asked was: "What happens to entropy when two gases like oxygen and nitrogen are mixed together?" The answer is that entropy increases, in fact, a formula for this increase is available. No problem so far. People then said that instead of mixing two different gases, let us bring together two bottles of the *same* gas and connect the two. Now, use the old formula to calculate the increase in entropy. A problem, immediately! If the bottles contain different gases, the formula works, but if the gases are the same, the formula does not work. This was a warning about the effects of particle identity, but people ignored it. Gibbs (a pioneer in thermodynamics and statistical mechanics) pointed out that the paradox disappears if one assumed that an error had been made in calculating $\Sigma(E)$, i.e., the number of states in a gas with energy less than E. This quantity $\Sigma(E)$ is needed while calculating the entropy of the gas. Gibbs assumed that the correct answer for $\Sigma(E)$ is $(1/N!)$ times the value calculated earlier. With this "fix", there was no paradox. This new rule of Gibbs, namely, that $\Sigma(E)$ should be divided by $N!$ to get the correct answer is sometimes called *correct Boltzmann counting*. Today of course we know better, thanks to hindsight, i.e., that the $(1/N!)$ comes as a result of indistinguishability.

4.5 Back to the radiation problem

With the benefit of all this hindsight, let us once again see what deriving Planck's law really boils down to. Recall that the problem is to find $\rho(\nu, T)$. For this purpose, Planck assumed that radiation was emitted by the oscillators in the walls of the cavity and that an oscillator of frequency ν transferred its energy to a cavity mode (i.e., radiation) of the same frequency ν. So, to find out how much radiation is present inside the cavity at temperature T and corresponding to a frequency ν, one had to first determine $\langle n_\nu(T)\rangle$, the average occupation number of oscillator of frequency ν excited to temperature T. It is in this step that one has to maximise entropy etc.

If we want to derive Planck's formula today, we will not follow the oscillator route described above. Rather, we would follow Bose, and what Bose did should become clearer, based on what I have said so far in this chapter. He does not mess around with oscillators etc. By 1923 Compton had clearly established the reality of the photon and so this was the starting point for him.

Bose goes about his business as follows:

1. First he divides the phase space into tiny cells of volume h^3 each.
2. Next he computes the number A_ν of such cells available for occupation by photons of frequency ν.
3. He then distributes these photons into the A_ν cells, quietly *assuming that photons are indistinguishable*. In fact, he calculates W assuming that photons are not only indistinguishable but also that there is no restriction to how many of them can be packed into one cell.
4. Next comes the job of maximising W which is necessary if radiation is to be in equilibrium inside the cavity.

All this finally leads to the result

$$\langle n_\nu(T) \rangle = \frac{1}{e^{h\nu/k_BT} - 1} .$$

According to Einstein, the energy of a photon of frequency ν is $h\nu$. So the average energy at temperature T associated with a radiation state of frequency ν is $h\nu \langle n_\nu(T) \rangle$. There are $g(\nu)d\nu$ states in the cavity between frequencies ν and $(\nu + d\nu)$. By the way, we must not forget photon spin and must remember to toss in a factor of 2 as Bose carefully did. All this gives us

$$\rho(\nu, T) = 2 \cdot \frac{4\pi\nu^2}{c^3} d\nu \frac{1}{e^{h\nu/k_bT} - 1} \cdot h\nu$$

$$= \frac{8\pi h\nu^3}{c^3} \cdot \frac{1}{e^{h\nu/k_BT} - 1} \cdot d\nu$$

which is the result sought after. This is a cleanly derived result, obtained by focusing entirely on the photons inside the cavity.

You might wonder whether it is proper to summarily dismiss Planck's oscillators as we have done above. In other words, should we not give some consideration to *where* the radiation filling the cavity came from? This is a fair question, and indeed in 1916 Einstein rederived Planck's law assuming that atoms emitted the radiation and that they did so according to the Bohr model. Interestingly, Bose extended this work of Einstein; that story comes in Chapter 6.

I am sorry I have had to go back and forth in my explanation of Bose's work. This is partly because so many different concepts are involved, besides which I am trying to set everything in a historical perspective. I realise I have not yet said anything worthwhile about the mysterious entity called *spin*. I hasten to rectify this omission in the next chapter.

Appendix to Chapter 4

Some useful results concerning permutations and combinations

A Let us say there are N distinguishable objects $a, b, c, \ldots$ We arrange them in different ways like $(a, b, c, d, \ldots)$, $(a, c, e, d, b, \ldots)$, $(e, a, f, b, \ldots)$, etc. Each arrangement is distinct from the other. The number of such permutations possible is $N!$. This is quite easy to see.

B As in **A**, we have N objects but must now arrange them in r groups or piles as below:

GROUP1	GROUP2	GROUP3	...	GROUP r
n_1	n_2	n_3	...	n_r

If $n_1, n_2, \ldots, n_r$ denote the number of objects in the various piles, then clearly,

$$N = \sum_i n_i$$

We now wish to find the number M of distinct piling arrangements. In doing so, we do not bother about the orderings within a pile. That is, if $n = 3$ and the objects are a, e and b, then we do not differentiate between the pile a,e,b, the pile b,a,e, the pile a,b,e, etc.

Suppose for a minute we did make such distinctions. In such a case, this problem is no different from the earlier one, and $M = N!$. However, we are overcounting if we do not make the distinctions referred to. If, for example, $n_1 = 3$, then, there are $n_1! = 3! = 6$ different arrangements possible in pile 1 and, in evaluating M we are treating these as different. To correct for this, we must divide the M value calculated above (i.e., $N!$) by $n_1 = 6$. Similarly, to knock off the overcounting associated with pile 2, we must divide by $n_2!$, and so on. Thus,

$$M = \frac{N!}{n_1!\, n_2!\, n_3! \ldots n_r!} \tag{1}$$

This result will come in handy when we deal with the Boltzmann case.

C Observe that when we regard e,a,b, (in **B**) as being equivalent to the arrangement a,b,e, etc., we are treating the objects as if they were *indistinguishable*. In other words,

> M also represents the number of arrangements of N things organised into r piles or groups or classes, members of each class being alike.

You will recall that when Bose distributed photons amongst the various cells, he used this line of argument.

D The number of ways in which m objects can be selected from a set of n objects ($m < n$) is given by

$$\frac{n!}{m! \cdot (n-m)!} \tag{2}$$

This immediately follows from (1) if we imagine that $r = 2$ and that the first pile has m objects. One often writes ${}^{n}C_{m}$ for the quantity (2) and refers to it as the number of combinations of n things taken m at a time.

Formula (2) also provides the answer to another apparently different question. Suppose there are n boxes and that m ($< n$) *indistinguishable* objects are to be placed in these boxes such that no box contains more than 1 object. You can convince yourself that the number of ways this can be done is given by (2). If you have guessed that this has something to do with the distribution of Fermions, then you are right!

E A slight twist to the case just considered. We have again n boxes and m indistinguishable objects ($m < n$). But this time we place no restrictions on how many objects can be put into a box. The number of ways in which this can be done is equal to

$$^{(n+m-1)}C_{(n-1)} = \left\{ \frac{(n+m-1)!}{(n-1)!m!} \right\} \tag{3}$$

This clearly has relevance to the Boson case.

F Let us now apply the above results to the general problem depicted in Fig. 4.1. Consider first what happens in, say, the ith cell. There are n_i particles distributed amongst g_i levels, all having the same energy ε_i. If the particles are Fermions, then we cannot have more than one in each level. In the case of Bosons there is no such restriction but we do have to remember that the particles are indistinguishable. For Boltzmann particles, even this restriction is removed. Remembering all this, we find that Fermions can have

$$w_i = \frac{g_i!}{n_i!(g_i - 1)!} \tag{4}$$

distinct arrangements in cell i. Thus, W, the total number of arrangements is given by

$$W = w_1 \cdot w_2 \cdot w_3 \ldots = \prod_i w_i = \prod_i \frac{g_i}{n_i!(g_i - 1)!} \tag{5}$$

Similarly, for Bosons we have

$$w_i = \frac{(g_i + n_i - 1)!}{n_i!(g_i - 1)!} \tag{6}$$

leading to

$$W = \prod_i \frac{(g_i + n_i - 1)!}{n_i!(g_i - 1)!} \tag{7}$$

We now turn to the Boltzmann case. If we do not look into the cells and simply ask how the particles may be arranged into piles, then clearly the number of arrangements possible is
$N! / (n_1!n_2!n_3! \ldots n_r!)$
However, let us now look closely into each cell—say, cell i for a start. Here g_i levels are grouped together. Thus, every particle when it is introduced into the cell has a pick of g_i choices. Thus there are $(g_i)^{n_i}$ arrangements possible inside the cell i. Taking this into account, we have

$$W = N! \frac{(g_1)^{n_1} \cdot (g_2)^{n_2} \cdot \ldots \cdot (g_r)^{n_r}}{n_1!\, n_2! \ldots n_r!}$$

$$= N! \prod_i \frac{(g_i)^{n_i}}{n_i!} \tag{8}$$

Now, it turns out that in many problems the factor $N!$ in (8) can be dropped (since it will cancel out when certain averages are calculated). Alternately, one divides the result for W as given by (8) by $(1/N!)$. This is referred to in section 4.4. So one writes W in a standard form as

$$W = \prod_i w_i = \prod_i \frac{(g_i)^{n_i}}{n_i!} \tag{9}$$

Caution: The factor $N!$ cannot always be dropped.

5 *Spin And Statistics*

5.1 Introduction

In Chapter 2, I introduced a mysterious quantity named spin and left you wondering about it. This so-called spin refers to an *intrinsic* angular momentum, and permits a distinction between Bosons and Fermions. Spin is characterised by a quantum number s called the *spin quantum* number, the associated spin angular momentum being $s\hbar$. Quantum numbers have been known from the time of the Bohr model of the atom and, if you recall, the *principal quantum* number n (which Bohr introduced) could take on only integer values 0, 1, 2, ... The spin quantum number s, on the other hand, can take values (0, 1/2, 1, 3/2, 2, 5/2, . . .). Particles with $s = 0, 1, 2, \ldots$ are called *Bosons* while particles with s = 1/2, 3/2, 5/2, . . . are referred to as *Fermions*—this identification is partly the result of experience

What exactly is spin? Why do particles of integer spin behave one way while particles of half-odd integer spin behave in another? Time to say something about these questions. Since it is all linked with quantum mechanics, a part of this chapter would revolve around early developments in quantum mechanics.

5.2 About wave functions

We will start with Erwin Schroedinger who, you remember, discovered wave mechanics. In wave mechanics, the central quantity is the wave function, and the aim of the game is to find out this wave function for the system one is interested in—the system could be as small as a single hydrogen atom or as large as a gas of helium atoms (which means one is dealing with as many as ~ 10^{23} atoms). Once the wave function is known, the problem is solved to a great extent in that many things we want to know about the system can then be calculated (at least in principle) in a straight forward fashion. The problem of course is to find the wave function, which one does by solving the *Schroedinger equation.* By the way, solving this equation is more easily said than done!

When wave mechanics was first proposed, people did not quite know what exactly the wave function represented. That, however, soon became clear thanks to Max Born. Let me give you two examples by way of explaining Born's idea. Consider a particle moving in one dimension. The wave function for this particle is written as $\psi(x)$, where x is the space coordinate and can take any value between $-\infty$ and $+\infty$. The quantity $\psi(x)$ denotes the *wave amplitude* at the point x. For a free particle, the Schroedinger equation is trivial to solve and the solution is

$$\psi(x) = Ae^{ikx} = A \cos kx + i \cdot A \sin kx$$

where A is a suitable constant. The quantity k is called the wave vector. Recall that according to de Broglie, matter could behave both as a particle and as a wave. De Broglie showed that the wavelength λ associated with a particle of mass m and moving with a velocity v is given by

$$\lambda = \frac{h}{mv} \tag{5.1}$$

λ is called the *de Broglie wavelength* of the particle. The wave vector $k = (2\pi/\lambda)$.

In general, the wave function $\psi(x)$ is a complex quantity, as it is in the above example. Born said $|\psi(x)|^2 dx = \psi(x)\, \psi^*(x) dx$ ($\psi^*(x)$ is the complex conjugate of $\psi(x)$, and in this case equals $A^* e^{-ikx}$) *denotes the probability of finding the particle between x and x + dx.*

Now for the second example which deals with a scattering problem. Suppose there is a pond in which the water is very still. There is also a pole stuck in the pond and which is projecting out of the water surface. Say a pebble is now dropped into the pond. Naturally ripples would be generated, and when they reach the pole, secondary ripples would also be generated as illustrated in Fig. 5.1. In modern language, we would say that the pole *scatters* the waves incident on it.

Scattering problems are very common in physics as scattering provides a convenient means of studying the properties of physical systems. The general idea is to shoot projectiles at the system under study and see how these projectiles bounce off. And the way they scatter, tells us something about the system they are bouncing off from. The scattered particles are like spies! You might remember that Rutherford discovered the nucleus of the atom via scattering experiments.

How does one describe scattering in quantum mechanics? Obviously via the wave function. And how is the wave function related to what one observes in an experiment? This is what I wish to briefly explain now.

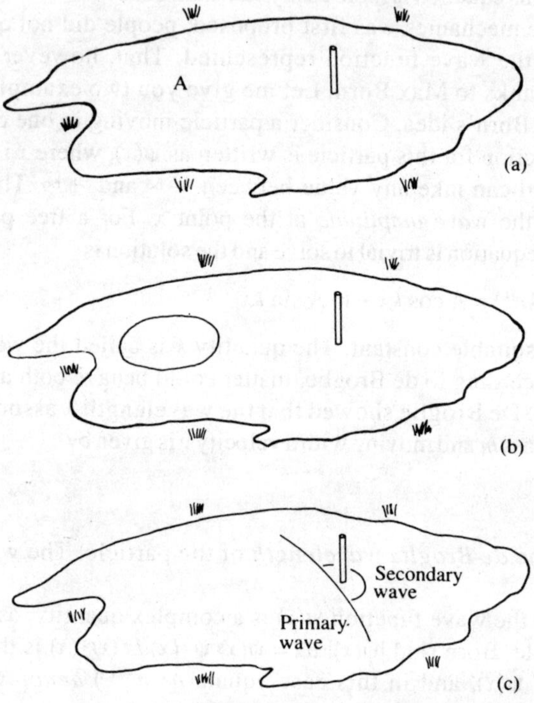

Fig. 5.1 (a) shows a still pond in which there is a pole. A pebble is dropped at A which then produces a ripple as shown in (b). When the wave reaches the pole, a secondary ripple, wave or disturbance is produced as shown in (c). In scattering theory, this is referred to as the scattered wave.

The incident particles are described by a wave function which is usually written as (taking the incident beam to be moving along the positive z-axis)

$$\psi_{\text{inc}} \sim e^{ikz}$$

The scattered wave function has the form

$$\psi_{\text{sc}} \sim f(\theta) \cdot (e^{ikr}/r)$$

See Fig. 5.2. The quantity $f(\theta)$ (in general complex) contains some information about the scattering system and is referred to as the *scattering amplitude*. In a scattering experiment, one measures how many particles are scattered in a given direction when a certain number of particles are incident on the system. The number of particles scattered between the angles θ and $\theta + d\theta$ is proportional to

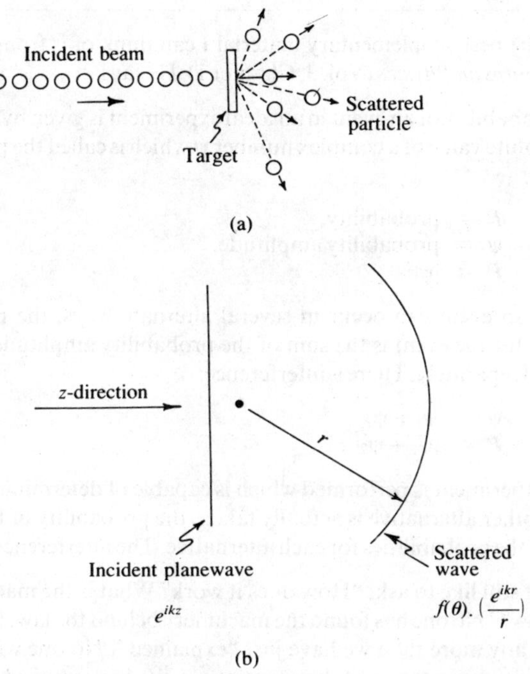

Fig. 5.2 In a scattering experiment, one shoots projectiles at a target and sees how the projectiles are deflected in various directions. This is schematically shown in (a). In fact, it is from such an experiment that Rutherford discovered the atomic nucleus. A "quantum mechanic" would visualise the scattering experiment as in (b). There is an incident (plane) wave and a scattered (spherical) wave, just like in the pond example of Fig. 5.1. If one knows the amplitude of the scattered wave, then one could calculate how many of the incident projectiles would be deflected at any particular angle θ.

$$N \cdot |f(\theta)|^2 d\theta$$

where N is the number of particles in the incident beam crossing unit-area per unit time. So you see how the wave function enters into the description of scattering. So much for a glimpse of the wave function and its relationship to the probability of events observed. Some supplementary material may be found in Box 5.1.

5.3 Zeeman effect—normal and anomalous

We now turn to the spin business. When the Bohr model was first proposed it was a roaring success but soon it began to have all kinds of problems; some could be patched up while others could not. I am now

Box 5.1 The best supplementary material I can think of is from Feynman's famous *Lectures on Physics* (Vol. 3, Chapter 1). He says:

(1) The probability of an event in an ideal experiment is given by the square of the absolute value of a complex number ψ which is called the probability amplitude:

$$P = \text{probability},$$
$$\psi = \text{probability amplitude},$$
$$P = |\psi|^2.$$

(2) When an event can occur in several alternate ways, the probability amplitude for the event is the sum of the probability amplitudes for each considered separately. There is interference:

$$\psi = \psi_1 + \psi_2$$
$$P = |\psi_1 + \psi_2|^2.$$

(3) If an experiment is performed which is capable of determining whether one or another alternative is actually taken, the probability of the event is the sum of the probabilities for each alternative. The interference is lost!

One might still like to ask: "How does it work? What is the machinery behind the law?" No one has found the machinery behind the law. No one can "explain" any more than we have just "explained". No one will give you any deeper representation of the situation . . . We have implied that in our experimental arrangement (or even in the best possible one) it would be impossible to predict exactly what would happen. We can only predict odds! This would mean that physics has given up on the problem of trying to predict exactly what would happen in a definite circumstance. Yes! Physics *has* given up. *We do not know how to predict what would happen in a given circumstance*. . .

going to briefly describe one of the patching attempts which eventually led to the discovery of electron spin.

The story of spin has its beginnings over a hundred years ago when Faraday tried to see what happened to the spectral lines emitted by a flame when a magnet was brought near it. Faraday did not observe any change but that was because (i) the magnet he used was not powerful enough, and (ii) he did not have a good enough spectroscope to observe changes in the spectral lines. In 1896, Zeeman of Holland repeated Faraday's experiment and found that the spectral lines became somewhat blurred or broadened. In the following year he used better equipment and discovered that what seemed like a broadening earlier was really a *splitting* of the spectral lines—see Fig. 5.3. Such a splitting is now referred to as the *Zeeman effect*. The famous Dutch physicist Lorentz

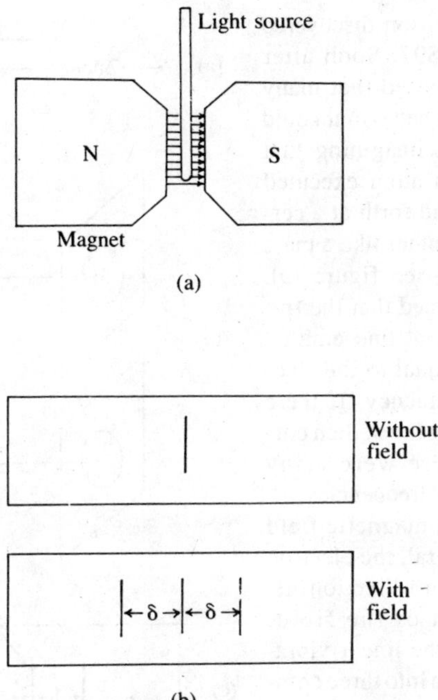

Fig. 5.3 The Zeeman effect refers to the splitting of a spectral line produced by a magnetic field. (a) shows schematically the experimental arrangement. The light source is placed between the poles of an electromagnet, and the light is observed in a direction perpendicular to that of the magnetic field. (b) shows sketches of the spectrum in the absence of and in the presence of the field. With a field, there are two additional lines (or satellites if you wish). The frequency shift δ depends on the magnitude of the applied field; the larger the field, the greater is the shift. With a weak field and poor spectral resolution, one would merely see a blur, which is what Faraday saw. Clear splitting as above was first seen by Zeeman.

immediately came up with an explanation for Zeeman's discovery which is discussed in Box 5.2.

Shortly afterwards, the French scientist Cornu found that the well-known *D*-lines of sodium are split by a magnetic field as illustrated in Fig. 5.4—no triplet this time! Such "peculiar" cases were promptly named *anomalous Zeeman effect*, and in a sense, the discovery of the electron spin was spurred by attempts to understand the anomalous Zeeman effect.

A model frequently used then was the so-called *vector model*, due to one Alfred Landé. Before discussing what Landé did to extend the Bohr model, let us, for a moment, go back to the Bohr atom model itself. You will recall that in this model, the orbits were labelled by a quantum number *n* called the *principal quantum number*—see Fig. 5.5(a). Bohr explained spectral lines as being due to jumps of the electrons in the atom

Box 5.2 J.J. Thomson discovered the electron in 1897. Soon after this, Lorentz proposed that many aspects of electron behaviour could be understood by imagining that the electron in an atom executed vibrations back and forth at a certain frequency ν, rather like a mass tied to a spring—see figure (a). Lorentz also assumed that the frequency of a spectral line emitted by an atom was equal to the electron vibration frequency. If there were many spectral lines, then correspondingly there were many electron vibration frequencies.

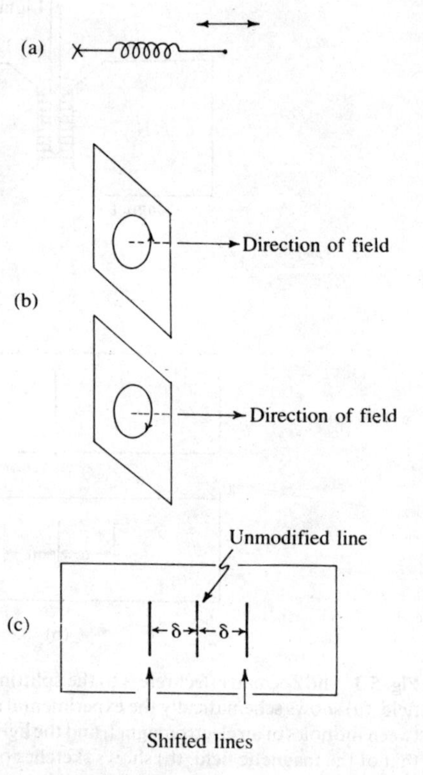

Now suppose a magnetic field is applied. In general, the electron vibrations may be in a direction different from that of the field. Lorentz resolved the linear vibrations of the electron into three components—(i) along the direction of applied magnetic field, and (ii) in a plane perpendicular to the magnetic field. The motion along the field direction was a vibration with the same frequency ν that existed before the application of the field. However, in the plane perpendicular to the field, the motion was circular—see figure (b). Actually, there were two kinds of circular motion, one clockwise and the other anticlockwise, their frequencies being

$$\nu \pm \delta = \nu \pm \frac{eH}{4\pi m_e c}$$

where e is the charge of the electron, m_e its mass, c the velocity of light and H the magnetic field. In contrast, the linear vibratory motion along the field direction produces a spectral line with the same frequency as before (i.e., an unmodified line—see figure (c)). This was how Lorentz explained the Zeeman effect. It worked alright but today we would explain it differently since we know that electrons inside atoms do not execute vibrations the way Lorentz thought they did.

between levels of different n. Later it was found necessary to take explicit note of the orbital angular momentum, which brought in

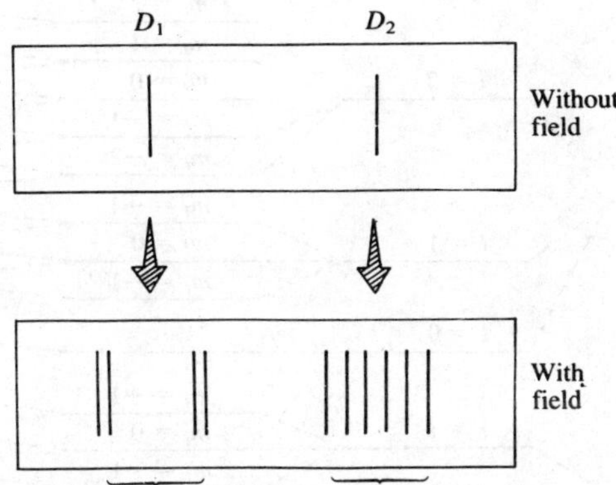

Fig. 5.4 Sodium lamps give off light of yellow colour. This light is essentially due to two spectral lines called D_1 and D_2 with frequencies rather close to each other. In the presence of a magnetic field, both these lines are split as shown. As you can see, there are more lines here than in the split pattern discovered by Zeeman (recall Fig. 5.3) which is why this case is referred to as the *anomalous* Zeeman effect.

another quantum number called the *orbital quantum number* denoted by the symbol l. Associated with a state labelled by a particular value l is an orbital angular momentum $(lh/2\pi) = l\hbar$. For a given n, l could take the values 0, 1, 2, . . . ,$(n-1)$. So the energy level spectrum got modified as in Fig. 5.5(b). Later it was found that each level corresponding to given values of n and l actually generated a cluster of levels in a magnetic field. To describe members of this cluster, yet another quantum number was needed— this time it was the *magnetic quantum number* m_l. For a given l, m_l could take the values $-l$, $(-l+1)$, . . . $-1, 0, 1$, . . . l. So, step by step, the simple energy level diagram of Bohr became richer and richer in details. In turn this meant that spectral lines would show all kinds of *fine structure* as well as splitting (when a magnetic field is applied). The fact that all these levels are there does not imply that the atom can jump from any one of these levels to any other; rather, there are restrictions known as *selection rules*. All this reasoning no doubt helped in understanding some of the complex spectra but an explanation for the anomalous Zeeman effect was still elusive.

One of the things that people realised soon after the Bohr model was proposed was that an electron going round in an orbit is like a current going round in a coil of wire. Such a current produces a magnetic field. Therefore, orbital motion should make the electron itself behave like a tiny magnet. On calculating the magnetic moment associated with orbital

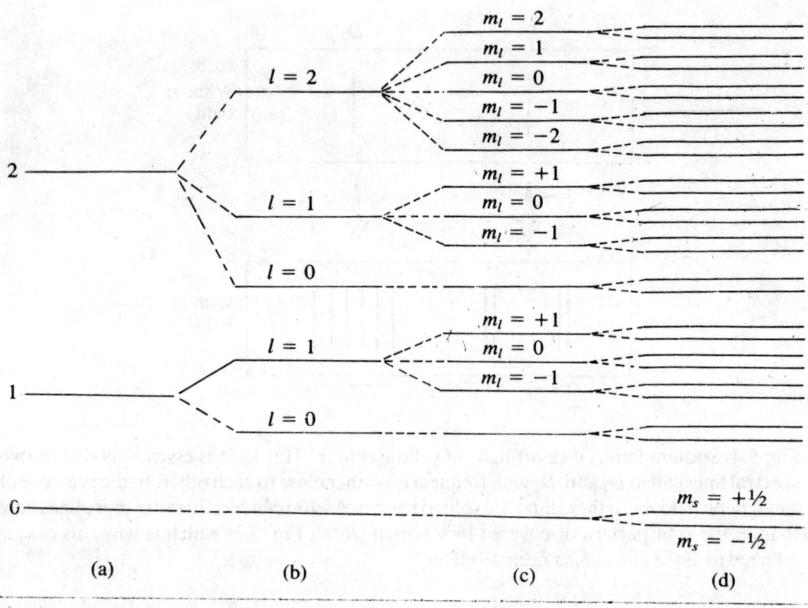

Fig. 5.5 Increase in the complexity of the structure of the energy levels of an atom. (a) shows the simple energy level structure proposed by Bohr, the different levels being labelled by the *principle quantum number n*. It was then found that the electron had orbital angular momentum, and that brought in the *orbital quantum number l*. Energy levels multiplied, and had now to be labelled by a pair of numbers (n, l) as in (b), which also shows the clusters born out of the original staircase of Bohr. Next people found that there was an *orbital magnetic quantum number m_l* which could take all values from $+l$ to $-l$. Correspondingly, in a magnetic field, the energy levels had to be labelled with three quantum numbers (n, l, m_l) as in (c). With the discovery of electron spin, one more quantum number was added to the list, and one now needed four numbers (n, l, m_l, m_s), with m_s taking the values 1/2 and −1/2 — see (d). In the entire process, the original spectrum of Bohr had become really rich in detail.

motion (the calculation is easy) it was found that the ratio of the magnetic moment to the orbital angular momentum is given by $(e/2m_ec)$ where e is the charge of the electron and m_e its mass. This quantity is called the *gyromagnetic ratio*. Landé however found that to obtain agreement with experiment, this gyromagnetic ratio had to be modified to $g.(e/2m_ec)$. This extra number g is somewhat like a fudge factor but it has a respectable name—the Landé g-factor. While some spectral splittings could be explained with $g = 1$, other situations called for values of g greater than 1. Why so? Nobody knew.

Meanwhile, Heisenberg proposed that the spectrum of the sodium atom (which has a core and one valence electron—see Fig. 5.6) could be interpreted by assuming that the core and the valence electron each had

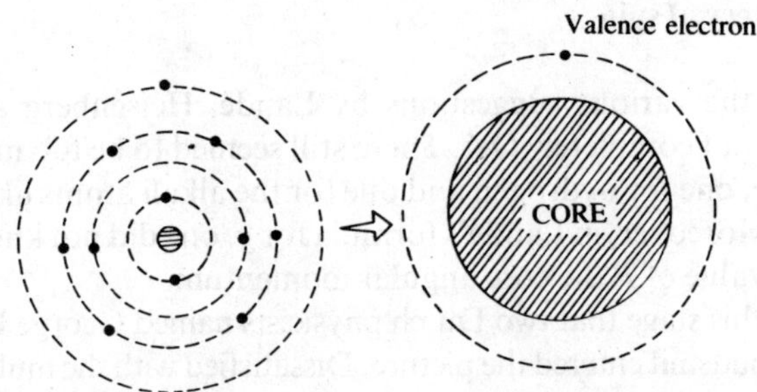

Fig. 5.6 On the left is shown the organisation of electrons in sodium into various shells. As shown on the right, the sodium atom can be viewed as being made up of a core and a valence electron. Landé proposed that the angular momentum of the atom is the vector sum of the angular momentum ($\mathbf{R}\hbar$) of the core and momentum ($\mathbf{l}\hbar$) of the valence electron. This gave rise to the vector model of the atom.

their own angular momenta which then combined in some fashion. Landé seized on this idea and declared that angular momentum being a vector, it obeyed the rules of vector addition to yield

$$\mathbf{j}\hbar = \mathbf{l}\hbar + \mathbf{R}\hbar$$

Here $\mathbf{l}$ and $\mathbf{R}$ are as defined in Fig. 5.6, and $\mathbf{j}\hbar$ is the total angular momentum of the atom. Working through a bit further, Landé then showed that g is given by

$$g = 1 + \{j(j+1) + R(R+1) - l(l+1)\}/2j(j+1)$$

where l, R and j are related to the magnitudes of the vectors $\mathbf{l}$, $\mathbf{R}$ and $\mathbf{j}$ respectively. Armed with this rule, spectroscopists soon became very busy. They were no doubt successful in interpreting all kinds of complex spectra observed by experimentalists but for Pundits like Bohr, Pauli and Heisenberg, to name just a few, all this success was quite mysterious because they were based on what seemed to be *ad hoc* rules. What was really happening inside the atom?

At this stage (i.e., around 1925), Heisenberg suggested that in addition to the previously known quantum numbers of the Bohr model, namely, n and l, a new one was needed. He called it R and said that in the hydrogen atom this new number R gave rise to a doublet, just as the l quantum number gave rise to a cluster consisting of $(2l+1)$ levels. The two levels in the doublet were labelled by the magnetic quantum number m_R. Pauli took the next step and observed:

> In a quantum state labelled by specific values for the numbers n, l, m_l, and m_R, there can be only *ONE* electron.

The Pauli exclusion principle had arrived!

5.4 Discovery of spin

In spite of the various suggestions by Landé, Heisenberg and Pauli, things were not completely OK. There still seemed to be too many rules, for example, one for hydrogen and one for the alkali atoms like sodium, and so on. Moreover, in Landé's formula for g, one did not know how to choose the value of R the core angular momentum.

It was at this stage that two Dutch physicists named George Uhlenbeck and Sam Goudsmit entered the picture. Dissatisfied with the multiplicity of recipes, they decided to look for something that would tie everything up neatly. And they succeeded. As Uhlenbeck wrote later, "It occurred to me that since each quantum number corresponds to a degree of freedom of the electron, the fourth quantum number [i.e., the R quantum number of Heisenberg and Pauli] must mean that the electron had an additional degree of freedom." And that degree of freedom is what we now call *spin*. It is as if the electron had an extra angular momentum $s\hbar = \hbar/2$ of mysterious origin. Be that as it may, the value of g for the electron now came out to be 2, in agreement with spectroscopic data. The discovery of spin by Goudsmit and Uhlenbeck together with the Pauli principle promptly restored order. One now knew how the electrons are organised into shells, and how these shells are filled in the various atoms. In short, one could understand the periodic table of elements. One could also calculate the core angular momentum $R\hbar$, the total angular momentum $j\hbar$, or whatever.

For a brief while there was the feeling that this new angular momentum arose because the electron was *actually spinning* about an axis. But there were problems with this picture; firstly, there was no way of understanding why the spin angular momentum was *half* $\hbar$. This half business was something totally new. Secondly, if the electron was actually spinning and also had a g value equal to 2, then the peripheral velocity (due to rotation) would have to be greater than c, the speed of light in vacuum which of course is not permitted by the theory of relativity. Soon people came to their senses and said that this new degree of freedom had *nothing* whatsoever to do with a spinning electron in the sense of *mechanical* rotation, but retained the name *spin* nevertheless!

Perhaps you are a bit dazed because I have been saying so many things rapidly. So let me briefly recapitulate. The concept of electron spin was discovered while people were trying to understand complex spectra. All kinds of rules were being proposed at that time, and while they worked in some cases they also failed in others. At this stage Goudsmit and Uhlenbeck discovered that if one supposed that the electron had an extra degree of freedom, then everything fell into place. This extra degree of freedom was called spin, and thanks to it, it seemed as if the electron had an extra or intrinsic angular momentum ($\hbar/2$) *over and above* any orbital angular momentum $l\hbar$ that it might have due to orbital motion. One now says that the electron has a spin angular momentum $s\hbar$, with the spin quantum number s having the value 1/2. Goudsmit and Uhlenbeck did not explain *why* there should be a spin degree of freedom and why s should have the value 1/2. They merely pointed out that once one assumes that electron spin exists, interpreting spectra becomes easier. Even anomalous Zeeman effect got explained, and the Pauli principle now had a clear meaning.

5.5 More about spin

We now take a minute off and focus on this extra degree of freedom. A particle moving along one direction, say the x-axis, has one degree of freedom (of motion). Likewise, we can have particle motion in two, and three dimensions leading to two and three degrees of freedom respectively. Consider now an electron with one degree of freedom. Its wave function can be formally written as $\psi(x)$. After the discovery of spin, this had to be changed to $\psi(x; \sigma)$ where σ denotes the extra coordinate corresponding to the spin degree of freedom. The interesting thing about this new coordinate is that unlike x, it can take only two values, $\hbar/2$ and $-\hbar/2$. In other words, σ is a *discrete* coordinate. Since those days when spin was first discovered, we have come a long way and many other new degrees of freedom have been discovered in the world of elementary particles. Thus, for the wave function of these exotic particles, one would now write

> ψ(x; spin coordinate; strangeness coordinate; isotopic spin coordinate; . . .).

Some of the new names like strangeness are fancy, aren't they?

Getting back to spin, its discovery was a landmark in that for the first time, one was dealing with a *nonclassical* degree of freedom. Soon it became known that besides the electron, other elementary particles also possessed spin, and that this spin angular momentum was either an odd or an even multiple of $\hbar/2$. Composite particles like the nuclei (which are made up of protons and neutrons) have a *net* spin which is the result of the addition of various spins—see Fig. 5.7 for some examples. (Actually, the quantum mechanical rule for the addition of two or more angular momenta is a bit more technical, but we shall not go into that here.) Atoms have a net spin which is determined by the spin of the nucleus, together with that of the electron system. Naturally, composite spin is also either half odd integral or integral. As we have seen, particles of the former type are now called Fermions while those of the latter type are called Bosons.

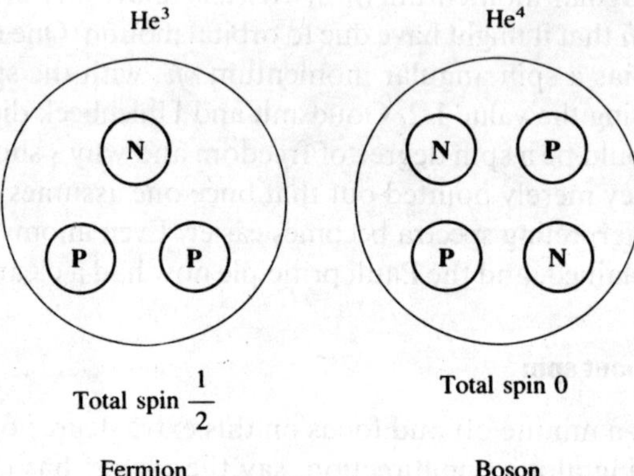

Fig. 5.7 Nuclei are made up of neutrons and protons. Both the neutron and the proton are Fermions, and a nucleus is a *composite* particle made up of Fermions. Such a composite particle could be either a Boson or a Fermion, depending upon how the individual spins combine. Two examples are shown.

5.6 Symmetry and antisymmetry

Heisenberg's paper (on the electron having a new quantum number R) which set Pauli and others thinking, appeared in July 1925. Goudsmit and Uhlenbeck discovered electron spin in October of the same year. In January 1926 appeared Schroedinger's first paper on wave mechanics. Six months later Dirac stated an important theorem relating to the behaviour of Bosons and Fermions. Some notation is needed before explaining that theorem. We suppose there are N *identical* particles—I mean if they are Fermions, they are all the same type of Fermions, e.g., electrons, and so forth. Let x_i, σ_i *denote the space and the spin coordinate of the ith particle. For convenience, we shall abbreviate* x_i , σ_i *by just i*, and write the N-particle wave function as $\Psi(1, 2, 3, \ldots i, \ldots j, \ldots, N)$. Dirac said:

> Interchange *all* coordinates of the particles i and j. Write the new (N-particle) wave function $\Psi(1, 2, \ldots j, \ldots i, \ldots N)$ as Ψ'. If the particles are Bosons, then $\Psi' = \Psi$. If they are Fermions, $\Psi' = -\Psi$. In the former case the wave function is said to be *symmetric* under the exchange and in the latter case *antisymmetric*. [See also Fig. 5.8.]

5.7 Spin of the photon

The last major event in the story of spin is the epoch-making paper of Dirac published in January 1928. In that, Dirac gave his theory for the

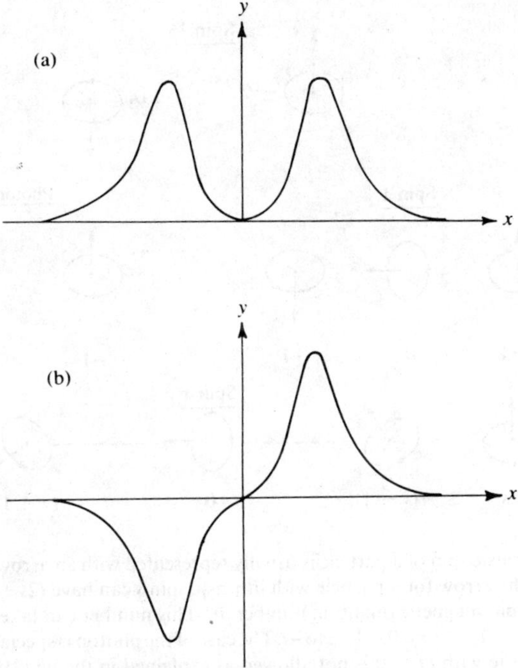

Fig.5.8 Examples of symmetric and antisymmetric functions $y(x)$. In the case of the symmetric function (see (a)), changing x to $-x$ does not change the value of the function while in the case of the antisymmetric function (see (b)), the value of the function changes sign.

electron. This paper went much beyond anything which had appeared before, and lo and behold, electron spin came quite naturally out of the theory! I don't suppose that overnight people had a better physical idea of electron spin but its existence was now a *natural* consequence of the theory; there was no need any longer to postulate it or anything like that.

Time now to say a few words about the spin of the photon. But first let us go back again to the electron for a moment. Like the orbital angular momentum, the spin angular momentum also makes the electron behave like a tiny magnet; in fact this magnetic property is always there, even if there is no orbital motion. Indeed, it is now believed that magnetism (of iron, for example) is the direct result of electron spin. The standard way of representing spin is to draw an arrow and make it point in certain ways with respect to a certain reference direction. For example, when an electron is placed in the magnetic field of the Earth, the local direction of this field could provide the reference. With respect to this, the electron would have two states as shown in Fig. 5.9.

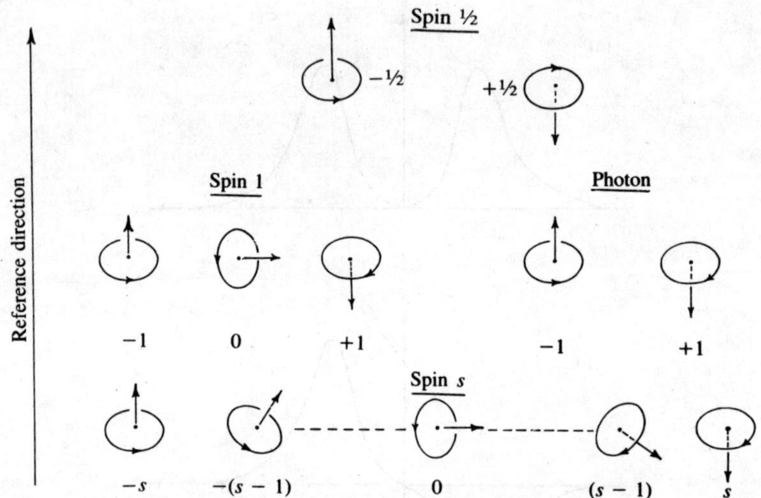

Fig. 5.9 The intrinsic spin of a particle is usually represented with an arrow Given a reference direction, the arrow for a particle with intrinsic spin s can have $(2s + 1)$ orientations labelled by the spin magnetic quantum number m_s. This number can take $(2s + 1)$ values ranging from s, $(s - 1)$, ... to 1, 0, −1, ... to $-s$. The case of the photon is special. Though it has spin 1, the substate with $m_s = 0$ is not allowed as explained in the text. In general, for a particle with spin s and travelling at the speed of light, only the two substates with $m_s = +s$ and $m_s = -s$ are allowed; all the rest are *NOT* allowed.

For spin 1/2, there are only two substates; for higher spins there are more. In general, for spin s there are $(2s + 1)$ substates and correspondingly $(2s + 1)$ orientations for the arrow—see Fig. 5.9. Notice that the orientations are defined with respect to a reference direction. These substates or orientations could be labelled by a magnetic spin quantum number m_s which can take any one of the $(2s + 1)$ values from s, $(s - 1)$, . . . to $(-s + 2)$, $(-s + 1)$, $-s$. The quantity m_s is like m_l introduced earlier. In the presence of a magnetic field, the various magnetic substates of a particle would have different energies. Otherwise, the energies would be the same, i.e., these different substates would be degenerate.

Now the photon is supposed to have spin 1 whence one must expect three substates or 3 orientations for the spin arrow. Pundits have established a connection between photon spin and polarization familiar to us in optics. You might remember that light consists of transverse electromagnetic waves meaning that the electric field and the magnetic field associated with the wave are perpendicular to the direction of propagation as discussed in Box 5.3. If the electric field **E** remains all the

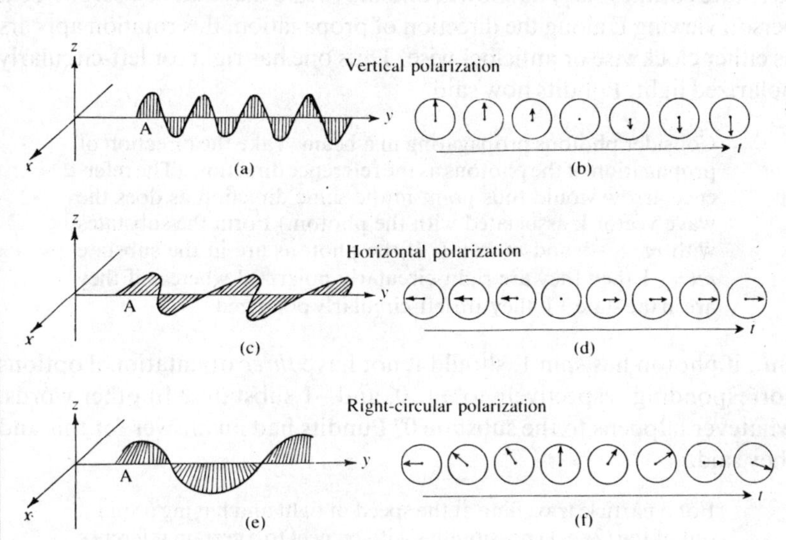

Box 5.3 Maxwell showed that light is nothing but a transverse electromagnetic wave, meaning that the electric and magnetic fields associated with the wave are perpendicular to the direction of propagation. In the figures here, only the electric field is shown (once that is known, the direction of the magnetic field gets automatically fixed). Consider (a). This shows the wave at a particular instant of time. The electric field vectors are all in the *yz*-plane and, in this particular case, are pointing in the *z*-direction. Such a light wave is said to be *linearly polarized.* If an observer were to concentrate on the electric vector at the point A, then what he would see at various times is shown in (b). We imagine that the observer is viewing along the *y*-axis. (c) and (d) illustrate an alternate scenario where the electric vector is along *x*. There are thus two independent possibilities for linear polarization, the vectors in the two cases being perpendicular to each other as in the examples of (a) and (c). In general, if the wave is going along the *y*-direction, these two polarization vectors could be anywhere in the *xz*-plane, provided they are perpendicular to each other. Light can also be *circularly polarized* as in (e). In this case, the tip of **E** vector spirals around the *y*-direction. What the observer at A would then see is shown in (f). He sees the electric vector rotating in a clockwise direction and therefore says that the light is *right-circularly polarized.* One could similarly have *left-circularly polarized* light. It turns out that these two states of circular polarization correspond, in the quantum language, to the two allowed spin substates for the photon shown in Fig. 5.9.

time in the same direction (therefore, this would also be true of the magnetic field vector **H** which is always perpendicular to the electric field vector **E**), then light is said to be *linearly* polarized. But it is also possible for **E** to rotate continuously as shown, and move like the head of a screw. To a person viewing **E** along the direction of propagation, this rotation appears as either clockwise or anticlockwise. Thus one has right- or left-circularly polarized light. Pundits now said,

> Consider photons propagating in a beam. Take the direction of propagation of the photons as the reference direction. (The reference arrow would thus point in the same direction as does the wave vector **k** associated with the photon.) Form the substates with $m_S = -1$ and $m_S = +1$. If the photons are in the substate $m_S = -1$ then they are right-circularly polarized whereas if they are in the state +1, they are left-circularly polarized.

But, if photon has spin 1, should it not have *three* orientational options corresponding respectively to +1, 0, and −1 substates? In other words, whatever happens to the substate 0? Pundits had an answer for this and they said,

> For a particle travelling at the speed of light and having a spin s, out of the $(2s + 1)$ possibilities with respect to a certain reference direction, only the spin substates $+s$ and $-s$ are necessary to completely describe the particle.

So, in the case of the photon which has spin 1, only the +1 and the −1 substates are needed; the one corresponding to 0 is not needed.

Here is an interesting point. When Bose did his work, he introduced a factor 2 which I have already mentioned. Like so many other things in his paper, he did this quite naturally. *This factor two corresponds to the two allowed spin substates of the photon*! Of course, Bose did not use the word spin, but its consequences were neatly and quietly taken care of by him. A few months later when the electron spin was discovered, people began to wonder about photon spin. The Dutch physicist Ehrenfest wrote to Einstein asking him to explain whether photon had a spin. Einstein was not sure. In his reply he wrote that he was not sure if "angular momentum could be maintained in quantum theory". This shows the confusion which prevailed at that time. See also Box 5.4.

May be at this point I should say a word or two about Raman's attempts to detect the spin of the photon. He did these experiments along with Bhagavantam around 1930 in Calcutta. Raman's experiments were not quite successful (although he thought they were—see Box 5.5) but what he has to say about the spin of the photon is interesting. He said (in his paper on the subject):

> In his well-known derivation of the Planck radiation formula from quantum statistics, Prof. S.N. Bose obtained an expression

Box 5.4 Years later, Bose discussed this *factor of 2* business with a visitor. In his paper, he had said that this factor came from the fact that the photon carried one unit of angular momentum and that this could only take 2 orientations. Bose added:

> But Einstein wasn't satisfied with that. The old man crossed this portion out from the paper and wrote to me saying that it wasn't necessary at this stage to introduce such a concept. He considered it would suffice to say that it came from the two states of polarization of light. But in those days the polarization of a particle didn't make sense.

The visitor then asked Bose if after the discovery of the concept of spin, he (i.e., Bose) had tried writing to Einstein claiming priority in discovering the spin of the photon. An amused Bose shook his head saying, "How does it matter who proposed it first? It *has* been found, hasn't it?"

Box 5.5 Raman's attempt to determine the spin of the photon by light scattering is quite interesting. First I must say a few words about light scattering itself.

Consider an atom as in figure (a), and let us suppose that a photon is incident on it. Prior to Raman people used to think that if the photon is scattered, all that happens is that its direction is changed. In other words, it was then believed that the frequency is *not* changed. Thus, according to this view, red light is scattered as red light, blue light as blue light and so forth. This is an old idea going back to Lord Rayleigh, and scattering occurring in this fashion is known as *Rayleigh scattering*. Lord Rayleigh also showed that the efficiency for scattering varies as the fourth power of the frequency (i.e., as ν^4) which means that blue light is scattered much more than red light. Raman made the discovery, now called the *Raman effect*, that light scattering with *colour change* is also possible. Of course Raman scattering is quite weak compared to Rayleigh scattering which is why people did not observe it for a long time until Raman by his clever and careful experiments drew attention to it.

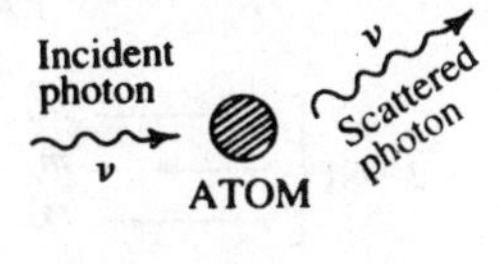

(a)

Raman scattering is a quantum mechanical phenomenon, and Raman argued that the scattering would be influenced by the spin state of the incident photon. He was right. Just to emphasise this, let us consider figure (b). This shows an atom in an excited state with the quantum number $J = 1$ and $m_J = -1$. When the atom de-excites, it emits a photon. The frequency of the photon would of course be equal to the frequency difference between the excited and the ground states. The question now is: "What is the polarization or the spin substate of the emitted photon?" It turns out that since angular momentum has to be conserved, the emitted photon would have to be circularly polarized, in this case right-circularly polarized. Similarly, if the atom were in the excited state $J = 1, m_J = +1$, the emitted photon would be left-circularly polarized.

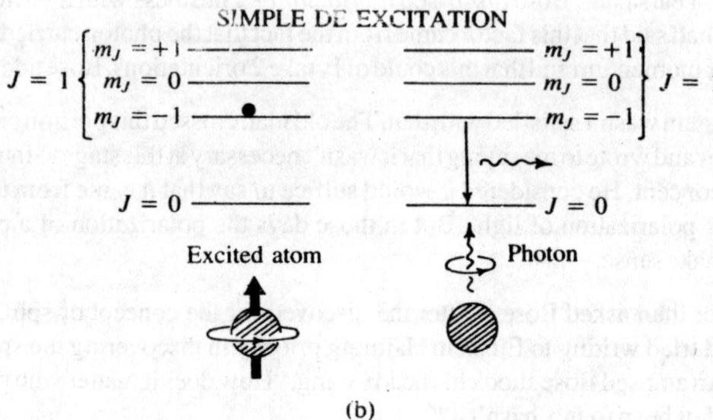

(b)

Slightly more complicated is the case of Rayleigh scattering illustrated in figure (c) where a right-circularly polarized photon is scattered by an atom in its ground state. The process may be regarded as involving two steps as shown in the figure, i.e., the photon is first absorbed and then emitted. At each step angular momentum is conserved, and, as a result, the scattered photon is also right-circular.

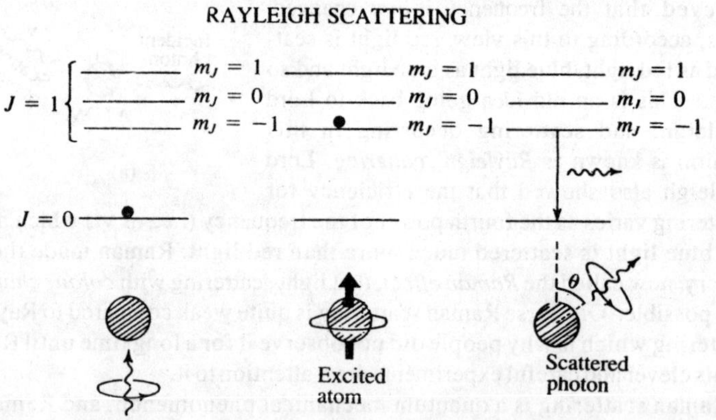

RAYLEIGH SCATTERING

$J = 1$: $m_J = 1$, $m_J = 0$, $m_J = -1$

$J = 0$

θ

Incident photon

Excited atom

Scattered photon

(c)

Raman reasoned along the lines of figure (c) and tried to find out what would happen if polarized light underwent Raman scattering, and if this could be used to demonstrate that the photon had a spin 1. Remember, arguments like I have given for figure (b) were not quite well known at that time. So Raman's thinking was quite original. However, the experiment he performed was a difficult one, and it did not quite work. But the attempt was good nevertheless.

> for the number of cells in phase-space occupied by the radiation, and found himself obliged to multiply it by a numerical fator 2 in order to derive from it the correct number of possible arrangements of the quantum in unit volume. The paper as published did not contain a detailed discussion of the necessity for the introduction of this factor, but we understand from Prof. Bose that he envisaged the possibility of the quantum possessing besides the energy $h\nu$ and linear momentum $h\nu/c$ also an intrinsic spin or angular momentum $h/2\pi$ round an axis parallel to the direction of its motion. The weight factor 2 thus arises from the possibility of the quantum being either right-handed or left-handed, corresponding to the two alternative signs of the angular momentum.

This again shows that Bose was quite clear about the photon spin concept if not at the time he wrote his paper, at least some time shortly after that.

5.8 Why different statistics?

You might wonder: "Why is it that Bosons have one kind of statistics and Fermions another? What is the connection between spin and statistics?" Let me answer this by quoting Feynman. He says:

> We cannot give an elementary explanation. An explanation has been worked out by Pauli from complicated arguments of quantum field theory and relativity. He has shown that the two must go together, but we have not been able to find a way of reproducing his arguments on an elementary level. It appears to be one of the few places in physics where there is a rule which can be stated very simply, but for which no one has found a simple and easy explanation. The explanation is deep down in relativistic quantum mechanics. This probably means that we do not have a complete understanding of the fundamental principle involved. For the moment, you will just have to take it as one of the rules of the world.

Well, there you have it! I should perhaps add a little note here. Today one talks of Bose–Einstein (B–E) and Fermi–Dirac (F–D) statistics. The former essentially refers to the distribution (2.2) and the latter to that in (2.1). These labels give proper credit to the founding fathers of quantum statistical mechanics. It is interesting that three of the four people involved won the Nobel Prize; only Bose failed to. Not that he was never nominated. He was in fact nominated many times but the Nobel Committee failed to honour him. This happens at times, and the classic case is that of Mahatma Gandhi who was consistently overlooked for the Nobel Peace Prize. Of course Gandhiji was far above the Prize but I cited this example just to show you how those who give awards are sometimes blind.

To sum up:

- In quantum mechanics one deals with wave functions. It is a complex quantity and represents a probability amplitude.
- Experiments cannot measure the wave function directly; but quantities related to the *modulus squared* of the wave function can be measured (as also some other quantities of a similar nature involving combinations called matrix elements, which, in turn, involve products like $\psi^*(...)\psi$).
- The wave function for a particle depends on all the degrees of freedom the particle has, including spin.
- Historically, the concept of spin was discovered while Goudsmit and Ulhenbeck were struggling to evolve a systematic set of rules for explaining atomic spectra. They discovered that the electron had an extra degree of freedom, completely nonclassical in nature. This new degree of freedom was christened spin, though it had nothing to do with mechanical rotation of the electron.
- Later, when Dirac gave his theory of the electron, the existence of the spin degree of freedom emerged as a natural mathematical consequence.
- Soon it was found that other particles like the proton and neutron also possess the property of spin, and one learnt to distinguish two broad categories namely Fermions and Bosons.
- People also realised the effect spin has on the wave function. The wave function for a many-particle system composed of identical particles is symmetric with respect to the exchange (of all coordinates) of a pair if the particles are identical Bosons and antisymmetric with respect to such an exchange (of all coordinates) if the particles are identical Fermions.
- For a particle of spin s, there are $(2s + 1)$ substates, provided the particle is not travelling at the speed of light.
- For a particle of spin s travelling at the speed of light, only the $+s$ and $-s$ substates of the possible set of $(2s + 1)$ such states need be considered.
- Particles with half odd integer spin obey F–D statistics and particles with integer spin obey B–E statistics.
- The connection between spin and statistics is rooted in relativistic quantum field theory.

6 *The Photon Story Continued*

Bose played an important role in our understanding of the photon. Part of this story was narrated in Chapter 3; I continue and complete the photon story here. But before I begin, I would like to quote Richard Feynman who says:

> Quantum mechanics is the description of the behaviour of matter and light in all its details and, in particular, of the happenings on an atomic scale. Things on a very small scale behave like nothing you have any direct experience about. They do not behave like waves, they do not behave like particles, or billiard balls, or weight on springs, or anything like that you have ever seen.
>
> Newton thought that light was made up of particles but then it was discovered that it behaves like a wave. Later, however, (in the beginning of the 20th century), it was found that light did indeed sometimes behave like a particle. Historically, the electron, for example, was thought to behave like a particle, and then it was found that in many respects it behaved like a wave. So it really behaves like neither. Now we have given up. We say: "It is like *neither*."
>
> There is one lucky break however—electrons behave just like light. The quantum behaviour of atomic objects (electrons, protons, neutrons, photons and so on) is the same for all, they are all 'particle waves' or whatever you want to call them. So what we learn about the properties of electrons will apply also to all 'particles', including photons of light.

Let me now go back to the year 1916 when Einstein derived the Planck formula in an interesting manner. Later Bose generalised this derivation.

Einstein had a go at the Planck formula because by this time (i.e., 1916), the Bohr model was available. It was thus possible to use a more realistic picture of the emission and absorption of radiation than the oscillator model that Planck had resorted to. Einstein said it is not oscillators which emit radiation but *atoms*, and they do so according to Bohr's rule

$$E_i - E_j = h\nu_{ij} \quad (6.1)$$

See Fig. 6.1. In his analysis, Einstein considered just two atomic levels, i.e., 0 and 1 (unlike in Fig. 6.1 where we have many levels). So only the transitions 0 → 1 and 1 → 0 were considered by him. Now an atom has to be in the excited state E_1, before it can jump to the lower level 0, emitting a photon of frequency ν_{10}. Once the atom has come to the level E_0, that's it; no more photon emission since E_0 is the lowest energy state. However, an atom in this state can *absorb* a photon of frequency ν_{10} and jump to the excited level E_1. Thus the atoms in the walls of the cavity are constantly jumping up and down in energy, depending upon whether they are absorbing or emitting radiation. If you focus on any one atom, you will find it changing its state randomly. You can't say in which of the two states it would be at a given time; however, since the walls of the cavity are maintained at a temperature T, one could say that the *average*

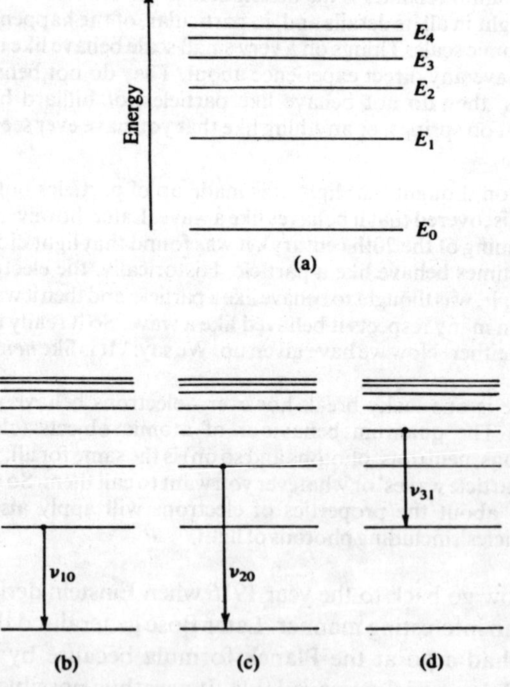

Fig. 6.1 (a) shows schematically the energy levels of an atom while (b), (c) and (d) illustrate various possible transitions being made by an atom from an excited state. The frequency ν_{ij} relating to a jump from level i to level j is given by the Bohr rule $h\nu_{ij} = E_i - E_j$.

number of excited atoms in the level with energy E_1 would be proportional to e^{-E_1/k_BT}; and this is what Einstein assumed.

As far as jumping up and down is concerned, Einstein recognised two kinds of processes—*spontaneous transition* and *induced* or *stimulated transition* (see Fig. 6.2). Now the upward jump $E_0 \rightarrow E_1$ can never be spontaneous; since E_1 has a higher energy than E_0, the transition has to be tickled or induced. However, the downward jump $E_1 \rightarrow E_0$ is a different story. The atom may simply get tired of sitting in the state E_1 and jump down on its own to state E_0 for a change. This would be a spontaneous transition. On the other hand, one or more photons (of frequency ν_{10}) might come along and persuade the atom to jump—this would correspond to *stimulated emission*. It is like, say, you are studying in your room and a couple of friends drop in and say, "Come on, let us go to a movie", and you go. You have been induced! So also, atoms can be induced. Thus,

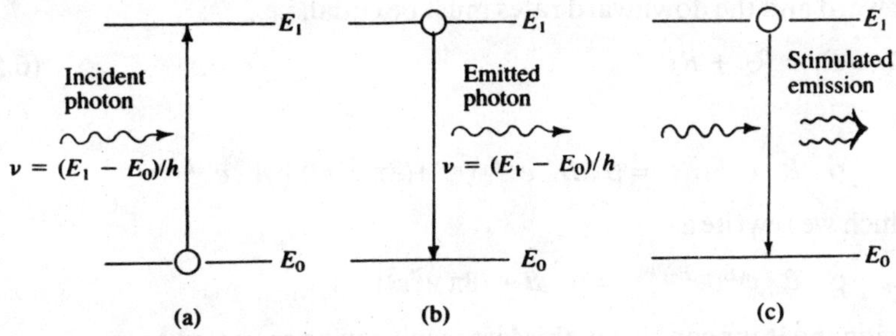

Fig. 6.2 This figure shows the difference between absorption, spontaneous emission and induced or stimulated emission. Absorption always takes an atom from a lower to a higher energy level as in (a). Of course, for absorption to occur, the frequency of the radiation incident on the atom must be correct, i.e., $h\nu$ must be equal to $E_1 - E_0$. Emission of radiation occurs when an atom makes a downward transition as in (b). The frequency of the emitted radiation is given by the Bohr rule. (c) also illustrates emission but under different conditions compared to (b). Here, while the atom is an excited state, it is exposed to radiation of frequency which exactly matches the frequency difference between levels 1 and 2. Under these conditions, there is stimulated emission of radiation as in (c). Stimulated emission can be strong in intensity and, as we shall see shortly, is made use of in the laser.

$E_0 \rightarrow E_1$ transitions, only induced.

$E_1 \rightarrow E_0$ transitions, both spontaneous and induced.

Clearly, for inducing a transition, the incident photon must have the right frequency.

In his analysis Einstein introduced two quantities A and B which are referred to as the A and B *coefficients*. The former is connected with spontaneous transitions, and the latter with induced transitions. Einstein then said that upward transitions occur at a rate R_1 (rate means no. of transitions/second) given by

$$R_1 = \rho(\nu.\ T) \cdot B \cdot e^{-E_0/k_B T} \tag{6.2}$$

Here $\rho(\nu, T)$ is at present an unknown function of the frequency ν and the temperature T. We shall find its form shortly.

Similarly, the rate R_2 for downward induced transitions is given by

$$R_2 = \rho(\nu, T) \cdot B \cdot e^{-E_1/k_B T} \tag{6.3}$$

In addition, there is a rate R_3 for spontaneous downward transitions given by

$$\begin{aligned} R_3 &= (\text{density of modes/unit vol.}) \cdot A \cdot e^{-E_1/k_B T} \\ &= (8\pi \nu^2/c^3) \cdot A \cdot e^{-E_1/k_B T} \end{aligned} \tag{6.4}$$

When radiation is in equilibrium, as it is inside the cavity, the net upward and the downward rates must be equal, i.e.,

$$R_1 = R_2 + R_3 \tag{6.5}$$

or,

$$\rho \cdot B \cdot e^{-E_0/k_B T} = \rho \cdot B \cdot e^{-E_1/k_B T} + (8\pi \nu^2/c^3) \cdot A \cdot e^{-E_1/k_B T}$$

which we rewrite as

$$\rho \cdot B \cdot e^{(E_1 - E_0)/k_B T} = \rho \cdot B + (8\pi \nu^2/c^3) \cdot A$$

Using the Bohr condition, this last result can be rewritten as

$$\rho \cdot B \cdot e^{h\nu/k_B T} = \rho \cdot B + (8\pi \nu^2/c^3) \cdot A$$

or,

$$\begin{aligned} \rho(\nu, T) &= \frac{8\pi \nu^2}{c^3} \cdot \frac{A}{B} \cdot \frac{1}{e^{h\nu/k_B T} - 1} \\ &= \frac{8\pi \nu^2}{c^3} \cdot \frac{h\nu}{e^{h\nu/k_B T} - 1} \end{aligned} \tag{6.6}$$

provided we choose

$$A = h\nu \cdot B$$

Notice $\rho(\nu, T)$ in (6.6) is the same as what we had earlier in (3.6). In other words, we have here a different method of arriving at Planck's law.

The above is a deliberately simplified derivation (adapted from a lecture given by Prof. E.C.G. Sudarshan) and is intended to convey the *spirit* of the game. Einstein of course carried out the derivation with care, although he made the somewhat artificial assumption that the atom had only two energy levels. Subsequently, he published another paper along with Ehrenfest wherein the atom was permitted more than two levels. The most important thing about this paper is of course the idea of induced or stimulated emission. This has important implications—(see Box 6.1). Concerning the factor $h\nu/(e^{h\nu/k_BT}-1)$ in (6.6), see Box 6.2.

Let us now turn to Bose's second paper on radiation in which he tried

Box 6.1 LASER is an acronym for **L**ight **A**mplification by the **S**timulated **E**mission of **R**adiation. The idea for the laser came from the MASER which stands for Microwave Amplification by the Stimulated Emission of Radiation. The maser was invented by C.H. Townes, and the operation of a simple three-level maser (or laser) can be understood with the help of figure (a). The levels shown might be associated with a molecule, for example.

Suppose we have a bunch of identical molecules, each with an energy level structure as in figure (a). Normally the molecules would like to be in the lowest energy state A, also called the *ground state*. Now let us suppose that somehow the molecules are all elevated to the excited state B. This can be done by a process called pumping—see (b). When excited, molecules like to shed their excess energy and go to lower energy states. Let us say this has happened and that a whole bunch of molecules have moved down to the level C—see (c). Suppose the decay rate from C to A is small. Then, thanks to the pump, a stage would come when more molecules would be in the excited state C than in the ground state A. At this stage we have what is called a *population inversion*.

The state C is not fully stable and so after a while, a molecule may jump down resulting in the emission of a photon. This photon would then tickle the other molecules up in the state C. In short, as explained in the text, there would be stimulated emission of radiation which, naturally, would be more intense than plain old spontaneous emission. Once the molecules reach the ground state, the pump puts them into level B from where they first descend to level C, from where they go back to the ground state by stimulated emission and so on—see (d). The cycle keeps going, building up the intensity. In effect, the signal (of light) is amplified, rather like the signals from a microphone are amplified by an electronic amplifier. If the frequency is in the microwave regime, one has a maser; if it is in the visible region, one has a laser. The first laser was built by Maiman of the Hughes Aircraft Research Laboratories.

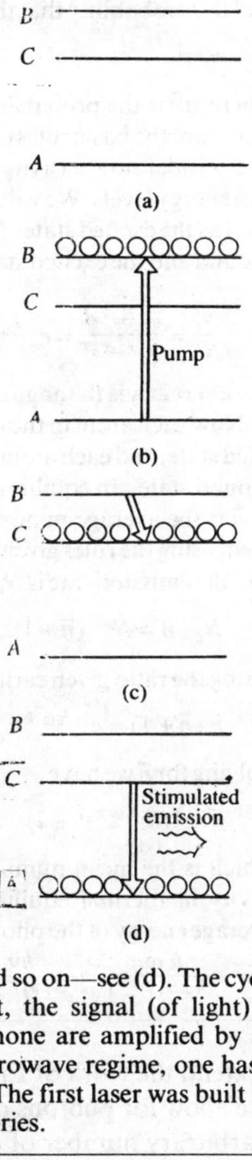

Box 6.2 Feynman gives a nice derivation of the factor $h\nu/(e^{h\nu/k_BT}-1)$ in (6.6). First of all, let us say there are n identical photons (all of same frequency, direction and polarization) in a box. There is also an atom sitting in the box that can absorb one of the already existing photons or emit another photon into the same state as all the other photons are already in. The probability that the atom will emit a photon is

$$(n+1)|a|^2$$

and the probability that the atom would absorb a photon is

$$n|a|^2$$

where $|a|^2$ is the probability the atom would emit if no photons were present. These are the basic rules of the game.

Consider now a cavity in which there are N atoms. Suppose the atom has two energy levels. We will call the lower level as the ground state and the higher level as the excited state. Let N_g and N_e be the average numbers of atoms in the ground and the excited states respectively; then at temperature T, we have

$$\frac{N_e}{N_g}=\frac{e^{-E_e/k_BT}}{e^{-E_g/k_BT}}=e^{-\hbar\omega/k_BT},\quad \hbar\omega=(E_e-E_g)$$

Here $\omega=2\pi\nu$ is the angular frequency.

Now each atom in the ground state can absorb a photon and go into the excited state, and each atom in the excited state can emit a photon and go into the ground state. In equilibrium, the rates for these two processes must be equal. If $\bar{n}$ is the average number of photons in a given state with the frequency ω, then, using the rules given above, the absorption rate for photons is $N_g\cdot\bar{n}\cdot|a|^2$, and the emission rate is $N_e(\bar{n}+1)\cdot|a|^2$. Setting the two rates equal, we have

$$N_g\cdot\bar{n}=N_e\cdot(\bar{n}+1).$$

Using the ratio given earlier for N_g/N_e, we then get

$$\bar{n}/(\bar{n}+1)=e^{-\hbar\omega/k_BT}.$$

Solving for $\bar{n}$ we have

$$\bar{n}=1/(e^{\hbar\omega/k_BT}-1)$$

which is the mean number of photons in any state with frequency ω, for a cavity in thermal equilibrium. Since each photon has an energy $\hbar\omega$, the average energy of the photons of (angular) frequency ω in the cavity is $\bar{n}\hbar\omega$, or

$$\frac{\hbar\omega}{e^{\hbar\omega/k_BT}-1}=\frac{h\nu}{e^{h\nu/k_BT}-1}.$$

to extend the work of Einstein which I have just discussed. Not only did Bose allow for photons of various frequencies and an atomic system with an arbitrary number of energy levels, but he also took into account the scattering of photons by electrons via the Compton effect. Pauli had earlier pointed out that this could be important.

At this stage, it is important to note that Planck in 1900 and Bose in 1924 deduced Planck's law by what Sudarshan calls a "static derivation using the notions of maximum entropy". Both addressed the question of radiation energy density in a cavity; whereas planck considered both material oscillators and radiation in his treatment, Bose was able to derive the final formula by restricting attention to photons alone. However, both ignored the fact that the equilibrium existing inside the cavity is the result of a dynamic process involving both the emission as well as the absorption of radiation quanta. In his paper of 1916, Einstein deduced Planck's formula via a dynamic approach, i.e., allowing for collisions between photons and atoms and permitting the atoms to make upward or downward transitions depending on whether they absorb or emit photons. There is a lot of give and take, and eventually there is equilibrium in the exchanges between matter and radiation. Of course, equilibrium means that entropy is a maximum but the point is that the derivation of the formula is not made by directly using the principle of maximum entropy; rather, equilibrium is demanded via the condition (6.5). Notice that whereas Einstein generalised Bose's first paper and deduced Bose condensation, Bose's second paper was a generalisation of Einstein's work done in 1916.

When Bose finished his second paper, he sent it, as before, to Einstein who once again forwarded the paper to *Zeitschrift fur Physik*. As earlier Einstein added a comment at the end of the paper, but this time he raised some objections. I reserve that story for Chapter 8. Here let me just say that this second paper of Bose has not attracted much attention. About this Sudarshan comments:

> It [this second paper] was as much a generalisation on the *A* and *B* coefficients of Einstein as was Einstein's paper on Bose gases a generalisation of Bose's derivation of Planck's spectral distribution law from the photon picture. Yet all these years and in all literature including the writings of Satyen Bose's contemporaries and students, this great contribution has been systematically ignored.

We now leave Bose behind and catch up again with the rest of the photon story. I have already pointed out that a photon is emitted when the atom makes a transition from a higher to a lower energy level. Where was the photon before that? It was not anywhere! It was created in the act of transition. Similarly, an atom absorbs a photon and goes up to a higher energy level. Where is the photon after absorption? Nowhere; it is annihilated. *Quantum field theory* provides a description of how particles (including photons) are created and how they vanish or are annihilated.

The history of quantum field theory is roughly as follows: In early 1927, Dirac showed how matter and radiation could be discussed together within the framework of the newly-discovered quantum mechanics. This was soon after his paper on F–D statistics. And then in 1928, Dirac decided to go beyond what Schroedinger had done and write a wave equation (for the electron) that took proper account of Einstein's special theory of relativity. Thus was born the famous *Dirac equation for the electron.* I have already mentioned that electron spin came out as a bonus from this equation. But there were also some problems, for the equation gave negative energy solutions. A free particle can have only kinetic energy, and kinetic energy is always positive. What on earth is meant by an electron having negative kinetic energy? Usually, when such a thing happens, one ignores the troublesome solutions by saying they are *unphysical*. In this case the solutions could not be dismissed so easily and one could do so only at the risk of contradicting quantum mechanics, which of course one could not afford. So, did the negative energy states really mean something unheard of before? If so, what was it?

For a while everyone was quite puzzled, with some people saying, "I don't believe in this whole business; there is something fishy here." Others offered all kinds of explanations. Dirac himself thought that the negative energy solutions perhaps represented the proton. Since the proton had a charge, opposite in sign to that of the electron, the sign of the energy would change and the problem would go away. But people were not convinced. The Dirac equation was for the electron. Where did the proton suddenly come from? Finally in 1933, Dirac himself found the answer. He said (in effect): "Listen, the negative energy solutions are no problem at all because they are all filled! So the electron cannot acquire a negative kinetic energy." Well, what happens if a negative energy state somehow happens to become empty? Dirac said: "No problem. An unoccupied negative energy state is like a particle, in fact it is a new particle which is not an electron. It has the same mass and spin angular momentum as the electron but the charge is opposite."

To put all this in slightly more respectable language which would not offend the Pundits, an unfilled negative energy state is a "hole" or a "vacancy state". But a hole behaves like a particle—see Figs. 6.3 and 6.4. It also emerged from the theory that a photon could, if it had sufficient energy, materialise into an electron–hole pair. This phenomenon is called *pair production*. According to the theory of relativity, a particle of mass m has an intrinsic energy mc^2 associated with it. This is called the *rest energy* of the particle. The rest energy of an electron–hole pair is $2m_ec^2$ which means that for pair production, the photon must have a minimum energy of $2m_ec^2$.

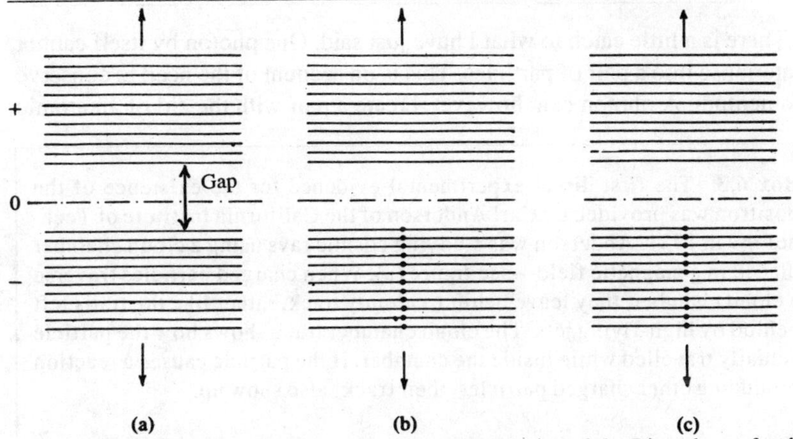

Fig.6.3 These figures explain what a position means, in terms of the Dirac theory for the electron. When Dirac first solved his equation for the free electron, he obtained both + and – energy levels as in (a). States with negative kinetic energy were an embarassment but he got rid of them by taking advantage of the Pauli principle and by saying they (i.e., the negative energy states) were all filled anyway, as in (b). What happens if there is an unoccupied negative energy state as in (c)? We now have a "hole state" whose behaviour can be understood with the help of FIg.6.4 Notice that there is an energy gap. Try to find out what it means.

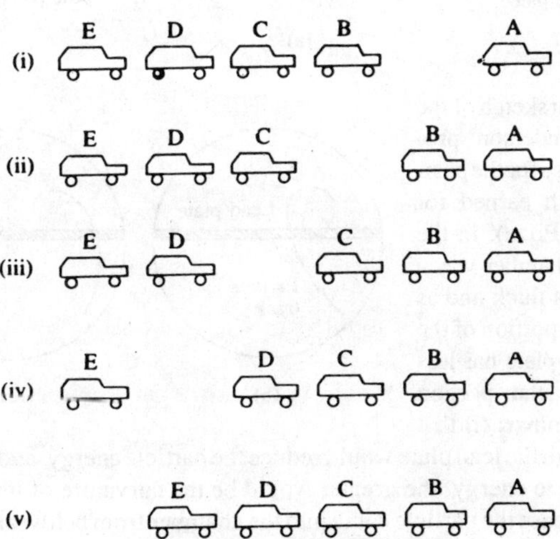

Fig. 6.4 Consider a line of cars as in (i), held up say at a traffic light. Noticing a gap ahead of him, the driver of car B moves forward to close the gap as in (ii). The driver of car C now notices a gap and moves ahead to close it as in (iii). This way, due to the progressive movement of the cars to the right, the gap itself moves to the left. In the same manner, a hole state can be regarded as associated with a new particle which moves in a direction opposite to that of the original particles. In quantum electrodynamics, hole states represent positrons (see Box 6.3) while in semiconductor physics a hole state is associated with a vacancy in the valence band.

There is a little catch to what I have just said. One photon by itself cannot materialise into a pair of particles. This is on account of the need to conserve momentum. A photon can, however, create a pair with the aid of an atomic

Box 6.3 The first direct experimental evidence for the existence of the positron was provided by Carl Anderson of the California Institute of Technology in 1931. Anderson was studying cosmic rays using a cloud chamber placed in a magnetic field—see figure (a). When charged particles traverse a cloud chamber, they leave behind a cloudy track, rather like the trails left behind by high-flying jets. The cloud chamber track shows how the particle actually travelled while inside the chamber. If the particle causes a reaction producing other charged particles, their tracks also show up.

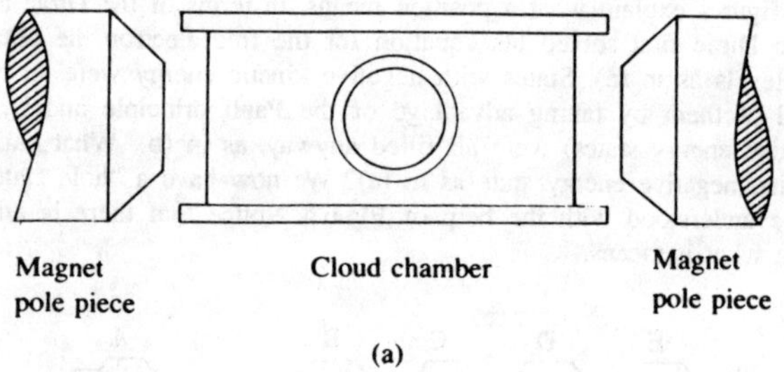

(a)

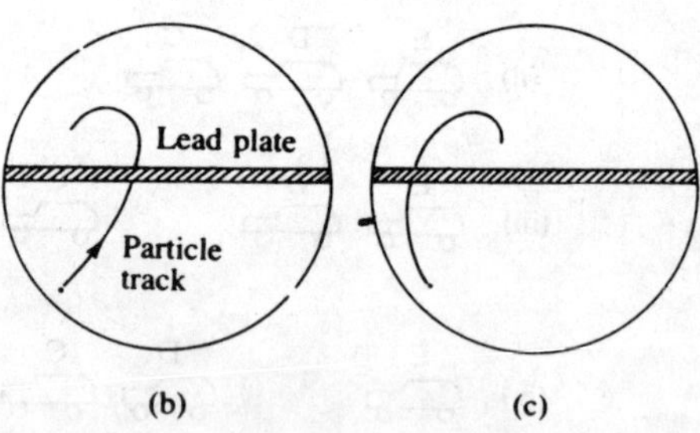

(b) (c)

Figure (b) is a sketch of the picture that Anderson produced as evidence for the positron (and which earned for him the Nobel Prize). In the middle of the chamber was a lead plate 5 mm thick and as one can see, the portion of the track below the plate has less curvature than the portion above it. One knows: (i) that traversal through the lead plate would reduce the particle energy, and (ii) that the lower the particle energy, the greater would be the curvature of its trajectory. Clearly, in this case the particle came into the chamber from below and travelled upwards. What about the charge of the particle? Using our knowledge of how charged particles deflect in a magnetic field, one can say the particle in this case must have had a positive charge. If the charge had been negative, the curvature would have been opposite as sketched in figure (c).

OK, so the particle had a positive charge. How do we know it was not a proton? From the curvature of the track, Anderson showed that if the particle was indeed a proton, it would have had an energy of about 0.3 MeV but such a proton would have left a much thicker trail than the one actually observed. More important, a proton with an energy of 0.3 MeV would have been completely stopped by the lead plate. So clearly the particle in question was *NOT* a proton, though it had the same charge as the proton. Other reasoning showed that it had a mass equal to that of the electron. As Anderson wrote, "It seems necessary to call upon a positively charged particle having a mass comparable with that of an electron." The editor of *Science News Letter* which published Anderson's discovery suggested that the particle be called the *positron*, a name which has stuck. Was Anderson influenced by Dirac's work? Anderson has this to say: "Yes, I knew about Dirac's theory . . . But I was not familiar in detail with Dirac's work. I was too busy operating this piece of equipment to have the time to read his papers . . . The discovery of the positron was wholly accidental."

nucleus because the latter can help with the momentum conservation business.

Soon after Dirac made this discovery, Carl Anderson in America produced experimental evidence that such a particle exists (see Box 6.3). We now know it as the *positron*.

You would think that by now all the problems had been solved. Not quite! The Dirac equation was designed to handle one particle but the solution seemed to suggest that there was an infinite sea of particles. So people went back and reworked the mathematical structure to take care of this new problem but all that is another story. The final outcome of it all is *quantum electrodynamics* (QED) which is the official name for quantum field theory which allows a combined description of electrons, positrons and photons. With QED, one can now describe Compton scattering, Raman scattering, emission of light from atoms, absorption of light by atoms—in fact all phenomena which involve light and atoms.

QED as it was formulated in the late twenties/early thirties seemed satisfactory and adequate, but only at first sight. A closer look revealed problems which were fixed independently by Schwinger, Feynman and Tomonaga in the forties. But all that is yet another story (see, *The Quantum Revolution,* Part II). Incidentally, this sort of thing goes on all the time in physics—most successful theories do a good job for a while and then run into problems, whereupon a new theory takes over. Sometimes the new theory is just a modification but at other times it is totally new. Both kinds are known. With QED there have been no problems since 1948. It has done wonderfully well and Feynman refers to it as the best theory we have today in physics.

Going back to Bose's discovery, it was really a part of a chain of important discoveries concerning the photon which started off with Planck in 1900. In the history of physics, conditions are sometimes ripe for making major discoveries. The period 1900 to 1930 was one of them. It is perhaps no accident that four major discoveries came from India during this period—first the discovery of *Bose statistics* by Bose, then the discovery of the *Saha ionization formula* by Saha, then the *Raman effect* by Raman in 1928 and finally the *Chandrasekhar limit* by Chandrasekhar, somewhere between 1930 and 1934. You might ask: "Have great discoveries in physics stopped? I thought more of them were being made. How come one does not hear anymore about similar discoveries from India?" Well, that question would require a whole book to answer. So not here please!

7 *Bose Condensation*

7.1 Ideal Bose gas

Earlier we have seen that Satyen Bose deduced Planck's law by regarding radiation not only as a gas of particles, but in fact as a gas of *indistinguishable* particles, now familiar to us as photons. We have also noted that as far as photons are concerned, their number need not be conserved. Einstein took the next logical step of considering a gas, the atoms of which, are indistinguishable and obey the same distribution as proposed by Bose in the case of photons. Now in a gas, the atoms are not annihilated and created the way photons are in a hot cavity (see Fig. 3.2). In other words, the number of atoms is conserved, and Einstein took care of that. Another important point—Einstein assumed that the atoms are completely *free* and do not either attract or repel each other. Such a system is now referred to as an *ideal Bose gas*, and has a very interesting property which I shall now discuss. Stimulated by Bose's paper, Einstein made this very important discovery now known as *Bose condensation*.

7.2 Bose Condensation

As you know, heat is essentially the random motion of atoms. The subject which deals with heat in terms of atoms is called *statistical mechanics*. I have already mentioned that prior to the advent of quantum mechanics, we had *classical* statistical mechanics (the founders of which include Maxwell, Boltzmann and Gibbs). Among other things, classical mechanics led to the result quoted in eqn. (2.4). For studying the Bose gas, we need *quantum* statistical mechanics.

Now the thermodynamic properties of a gas are obtained by studying what is called its *equation of state*. One of the objectives of statistical mechanics (be it classical or quantum) is to deduce this equation of state. Once this is known, one could then say many things about the way the gas would behave, for example, *when* it would condense. Let N be the number of particles and V the volume of the system of particles. It turns out that in statistical mechanics, when one wants to study the thermo-dynamic properties of real-life systems one must make both, the number N of particles and the volume V tend to infinity but in such a manner that the density (N/V) remains finite. Pundits refer to this mathematical operation as "taking or going to the thermodynamic limit". In this limit, one tries to obtain equations for (i) P/k_BT, and (ii) $v = (V/N)$ the specific volume (see Fig. 7.1). The *specific volume* depends on the pressure P, and so in a sense the equations for P

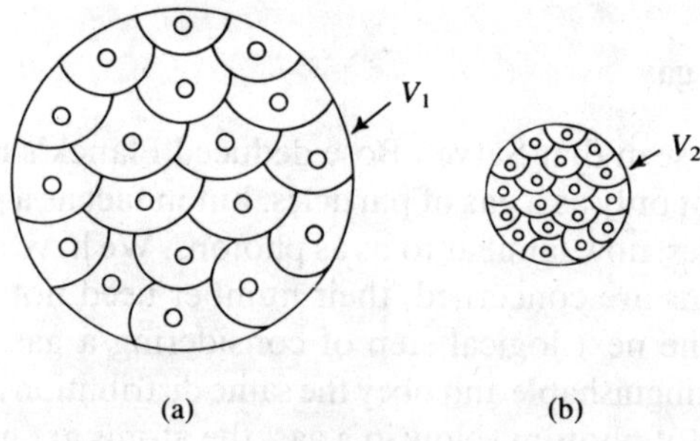

Fig. 7.1 Schematic drawing to show what specific volume means. In both (a) and (b) there are the same number of particles, i.e., N. However, the total volume occupied is different in the two cases, being V_1 and V_2 respectively. These spheres are partitioned into cells of equal volumes such that there is one particle per cell in the case of each sphere. The volume of the cell is called specific volume. Obviously the specific volumes v_1 and v_2 are not the same. From this one can conclude the following: Let $n = (N/V)$ denote the number density. Clearly, $v = (1/n)$. If r is the average spacing between particles, then $v \sim (4/3)\pi r^3$, i.e., $v \sim r^3$ or $r \sim v^{1/3} \sim n^{-1/3}$.

and for v are coupled. The equations are a bit complicated, which is why I have not written them down. Anyway, it is the physical concept which is more interesting, and so let us concentrate on that.

We know that in a gas, the particles can have all kinds of momenta and therefore all kinds of energies. Let us imagine that the energy states (or momentum states if you wish) available to a particle (in an ideal Bose gas) are as sketched in Fig. 7.2. Naturally, the state of zero momentum would be at the bottom. Since all the particles must somehow be distributed among the available states, we have

$$N = \langle n_0(T)\rangle + \langle n_1(T)\rangle + \langle n_2(T)\rangle + \ldots$$

$$= \langle n_0(T)\rangle + \sum_p{}' \langle n_p(T)\rangle$$

Here, $\langle n_i(T)\rangle$ means the average number of particles in level i at temperature

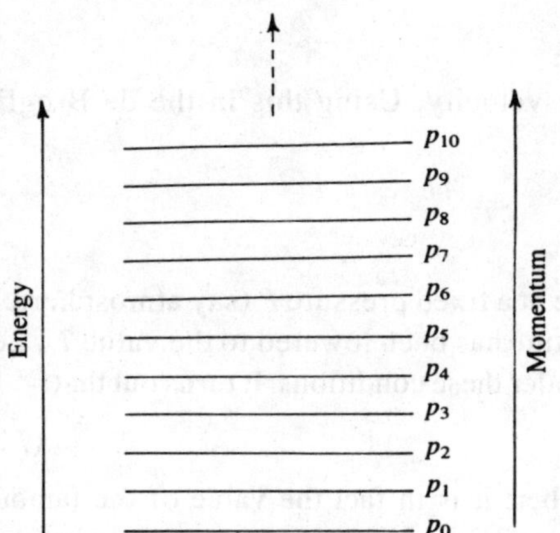

Fig. 7.2 Schematic representation of the momentum states of a free particle. The states are labelled $p_0, p_1, p_2, \ldots$, etc. Of these, the lowest state corresponds to zero momentum. In the text, p_0 is labelled 0, p_1 is labelled 1 and so on.

T, while $\sum_p'$ means that the $p = 0$ state is excluded in the summation. Therefore,

$$(N/V) = 1/v = \langle n_0(T)\rangle/V + (1/V) \cdot [\sum_p{}' \langle n_p(T)\rangle] \tag{7.1}$$

When T is large, the particles are distributed *sparsely* amongst the various available momentum states. No doubt the distribution changes with temperature, but basically the occupation of the levels remains sparse until the temperature is lowered below a critical temperature T_c when a *finite* number of particles suddenly drop into the state of zero momentum. I am sure you are both puzzled and worried by the terms "sparse" and "finite". Actually, these terms can be given precise meanings but for the present let us just say:

> Sparse occupation means that the number occupying is *negligible* compared to N while finite occupation means that the number occupying is *NOT* negligible compared to N.

Now why does the occupation of the lowest momentum state suddenly change from sparse to finite below a critical temperature T_c? What is T_c related to anyway? To explain this I must introduce you to the *thermal wavelength* of a particle. Denoted by the symbol λ_{th}, it is defined by

$$\lambda_{th} = (2\pi h^2/mk_BT)^{1/2} \tag{7.2}$$

where m is the mass of the atom. The thermal wavelength defined above is related to the de Broglie wavelength $\lambda = (h/mv)$ introduced earlier and is of the same order. Note that higher the temperature, the smaller is the thermal wavelength. At temperature T, one can take

$$\frac{1}{2}m\langle v^2\rangle \sim \frac{3}{2}k_BT$$

where $\langle v^2\rangle$ is the mean square velocity. Using this in the de Broglie relation, we get

$$\lambda \sim (h^2/3k_BTm)^{1/2}$$

which is of the same order as λ_{th}.

Let the system of particles be at a fixed pressure P (say atmospheric); we also suppose that the temperature has been lowered to the value T_c. Let v_c denote the specific volume under these conditions. It turns out that

$$\lambda_{th}^3/v_c = 2.612 \tag{7.3}$$

This 2.612 is not a magic number; it is in fact the value of the famous *Riemann zeta function* $\zeta(x)$ for $x = 3/2$. It all comes out neatly when the theory is worked out! If you want to know a little bit more, see Box 7.1.

OK, so when P is kept fixed and T is lowered, things begin to happen when T crosses T_c; suddenly, $\langle n_0(T)\rangle$ ceases to be negligible and becomes finite. More explicitly,

$$\langle n_0(T)\rangle/N = \begin{cases} 0 & \text{if } \lambda_{th}^3/v < 2.612 \text{ i.e. } T > T_c \\ 1-(T/T_c)^{3/2} & \text{if } \lambda_{th}^3/v \geq 2.612 \text{ i.e. } T \leq T_c \end{cases} \tag{7.4}$$

Box 7.1 The Bose condensation business is a highly technical affair, but perhaps I can add a word or two about the mysterious number 2.612 in eqn. (7.3). It all comes about as follows: To study what happens in an ideal Bose gas, one must basically examine the equation

$$\frac{1}{v} = \frac{1}{\lambda_{th}^3}\cdot g_{3/2}(z) + \frac{1}{V}\cdot\frac{z}{1-z} \tag{1}$$

where the quantities v, λ_{th}^3, and V are as defined in the text. z is called *fugacity*, and is related to $\langle n_0\rangle$ as we shall presently see. For small z, the function $g_{3/2}(z)$ can be written as the series

$$g_{3/2}(z) = z + \frac{z^2}{2^{3/2}} + \frac{z^3}{3^{3/2}} + \ldots \tag{2}$$

A graph of $g_{3/2}(z)$ vs z is shown in figure (a). At $z = 1$, $g_{3/2}(z = 1) = \zeta(3/2) = 2.612$ where $\zeta(x)$ is the zeta function. At this stage, the tangent to the curve is vertical (i.e., the derivative diverges, if you want to sound a bit technical). Note, however, that the value of $g_{3/2}(z = 1)$ is finite and equals 2.612. This is how this mysterious number 2.612 enters the picture. The fugacity z is related to $\langle n_0\rangle$ by

$$\langle n_0\rangle = \frac{z}{1-z}$$

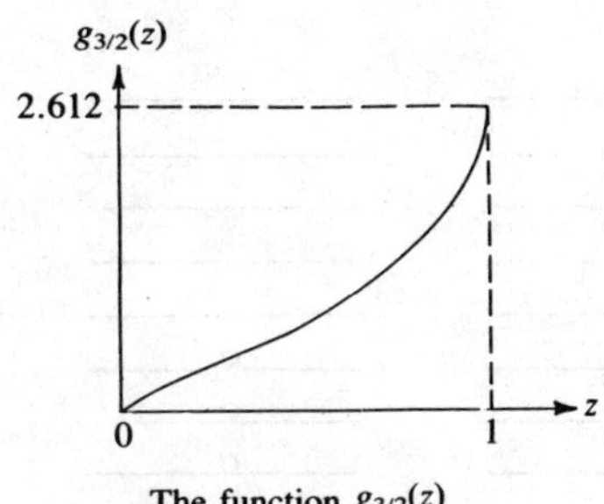

The function $g_{3/2}(z)$

In short, result (7.4) is obtained by analysing equation (1) above and using the series expansion given in equation (2). This analysis shows that there is a change of behaviour as $(\lambda_{\text{th}}^3/v)$ crosses the value $g_{3/2}(1)$, and that is what has been quoted in (7.4).

The *dramatic increase* in the occupancy of the lowest momentum state at T_c is referred to as *Bose condensation*. It is *as if* a gas has condensed into a liquid. Notice that not all the particles drop into the lowest state; only some (or better a finite fraction) do, and the rest are as before sparsely distributed amongst the various higher states. So it is as if there is a *mixture* of two "phases", a liquid and a vapour. It has been pointed out that gravity can separate this mixture into its two constituent components. Getting back to the condensation story, as one continues to lower T below T_c, the population of the lowest momentum state steadily increases until at $T = 0$, *all* the particles settle down into this lowest state—(Fig. 7.3). It is worth stressing that while Boltzmann statistics also predicts total occupation of the lowest energy state at the absolute zero of temperature, nothing like the dramatic increase in the occupancy of the lowest state at a *nonzero* temperature occurs within the framework of Boltzmann statistics.

7.3 Why Bose condensation?

Why on earth does such a "condensation" occur? The question is certainly meaningful because condensation of a gas into a liquid normally occurs on account of the existence of attractive forces between molecules or atoms as the case may be. In the present case, we have assumed the particles to be completely *free*, i.e., there is *no* interaction between them whatsoever. How come there is a condensation? Believe it or not. Bose condensation occurs due to the *symmetry property of the wave function*!

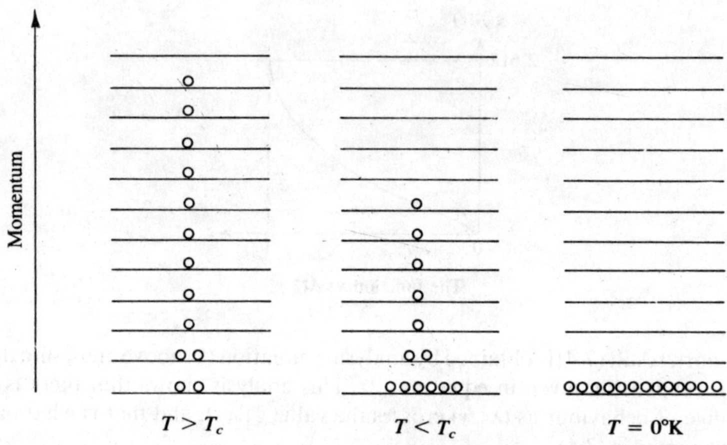

Fig. 7.3 Population of the momentum states of an ideal Bose gas at various temperatures. Above T_c, the population is sparse. Below T_c (but $T > 0$), all but the ground state are sparsely populated. The ground state alone is an exception, having a finite population. This means that the number there is not negligible compared to the total number of particles in the gas. This is Bose condensation, and first shows up when the temperature is reduced just below T_c. At T exactly equal to zero, all the particles comfortably settle down into the lowest state. But then this is an ideal that can never be reached!

What this effectively means is that Bosons, unlike Fermions, are not so shy and do not mind congregating in the same state—at least there is no Pauli exclusion principle to scare them away. Generally, Bosons like to go their "own way" so to speak, which explains their sparse distribution amongst the available states. But when the average interparticle distance becomes smaller than the thermal wavelength, the symmetry property of the wave function (recall Chapter 5) actually encourages the occupancy of the lowest state. You may say that quantum mechanical fuzziness and indistinguishability become important and lead to the condensation, particularly because disrupting effects due to temperature disappear. The wave function symmetry is an explicit signature of the Bose character of the particles involved. This is about the best explanation I can manage. Let me remind you again that after Schroedinger saw Einstein's paper he wondered about it and discovered wave mechanics (from which is derived the concept of the wave function). Bose condensation is essentially due to the symmetry property of the N-particle wave function, which was discovered even before the wave function was known!

Bose condensation was discovered by Einstein a few months after he had forwarded Bose's first paper, and was reported by him in a paper in early 1925. As he put it,

> A number of molecules steadily growing with increasing density go over into the first quantum state (which has zero kinetic energy) while the remaining molecules distribute themselves according to parameter value $A = 1$ . . . [This parameter enters Einstein's theory and was called by him as the degeneracy parameter]. A separation is thus effected; one part condenses while the rest remains as a 'saturated ideal gas'.

Even before he published this result, Einstein wrote to the well-known Dutch scientist Ehrenfest: "From a certain temperature on, the molecules "condense" without attractive forces, that is, they accumulate at zero velocity. The theory is pretty, but is there also some truth to it?" At that time the Pauli principle was not known, and Einstein thought that hydrogen, helium and the electron gas might be candidates for Bose condensation. Today of course we know that hydrogen and the electron gas are ruled out.

For some time, people thought that Bose condensation was a mere theoretical novelty but when an example was finally discovered, it proved to be a spectacular one.

7.4 The helium story

The helium atom has spin zero; a collection of helium atoms could therefore be expected to show Bose condensation. Einstein was therefore correct in supposing that helium was a candidate (however, at that time he did not know that Bosons ought to have integer spin, and much less that the helium atom was a Boson). There was, however, a problem with Einstein's suggestion—nothing peculiar happened when helium gas condensed.

Here I should perhaps say a word or two about the liquefaction of helium. Towards the end of the last century, there was a great race to liquefy all known gases (i.e., oxygen, nitrogen, argon, neon, hydrogen, etc.). Sir James Dewar was a great one in this business, and so successful was he that there was a little poem ridiculing his competitors:

Sir James Dewar
Is cleverer than you are
None of you asses
Can condense gases!

One gas which even Dewar could not liquefy was helium. This lone exception was finally tamed by Kammerlingh Onnes of Holland around 1900. The reason why helium was tough to liquefy was that it needed very low temperatures, much lower than that attained before.

Kammerlingh Onnes solved that problem, and so he was able to make liquid helium. And the temperature at which helium became a liquid (at atmospheric pressure) was 4.2 °K, the lowest temperature then known. See also, *A Hot Story*.

In 1928, Miss Keesom discovered that liquid helium underwent a phase change when cooled below 2.2 °K. (For more details about phase change, see the companion volume in this series called *The Many Phases of Matter*.) This transition was a most unusual one. Outwardly, the liquid appeared the same as at above 2.2 °K but it had some remarkable properties. In 1938, Fritz London proposed that the phase transition observed in liquid helium at 2.2 °K is an example of Bose condensation. Liquid helium below 2.2 °K is nowadays referred to as *superfluid* helium (see Box 7.2). The idea that the superfluid transition is indeed due to Bose condensation is now accepted, but there is a problem nevertheless.

Einstein showed that below T_c, $\langle n_0(T) \rangle$ became finite signalling Bose condensation. This result was derived by him for a gas of *free* Bose particles whereas in reality there is a certain amount of interaction between two helium atoms, i.e., helium atoms exert a potential on each other. So a gas of helium atoms cannot be regarded as free—in fact, the *liquefaction* of helium gas into a liquid is evidence that the system is an *interacting Bose system* rather than a free one. It turns out that it is quite a job to demonstrate Bose condensation in such an interacting Bose system, as also to derive a criterion as in (7.4), but Oliver Penrose and Lars Onsager have done that.

I cannot talk about liquid helium without at least mentioning the names of Landau and of Feynman, two of the great names in physics. Both of them have made very important contributions to the theory of superfluid helium but let me not get into that here. It would be too much of a deviation.

It is useful to summarise the cycle of events starting with Planck's discovery and concluding with Einstein's paper on Bose condensation:

1900 PLANCK:

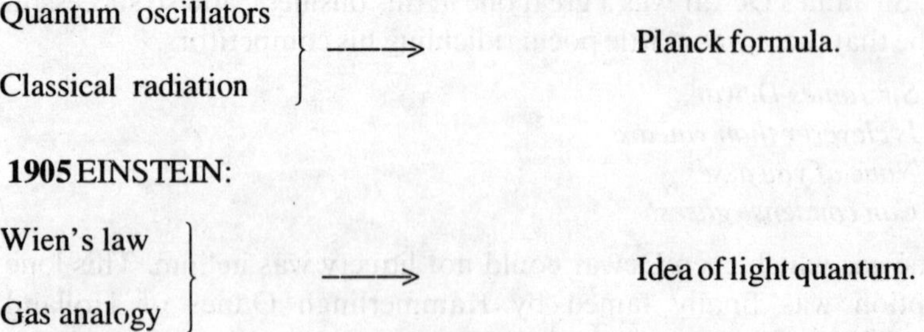

Box 7.2 It would take a whole book to describe all the fascinating things that happen when liquid helium becomes a superfluid, but two examples would at least give the flavour. Figure (a) shows two vessels, both containing liquid helium. A connection is made between the two vessels, the slit being very narrow. Above 2.2 °K the liquid flows from the inner to the outer vessel with great difficulty whereas, below that temperature, the liquid flows very rapidly from the inner to the outer vessel till the levels in the two become equal. It is as if the liquid has no viscosity; hence the term *superfluidity*. Another example of the strange behaviour of superfluid helium is shown in figure (b). Here there are two vessels one large and one small, both containing liquid helium below 2.2 °K. A very thin layer of liquid helium forms, and the film creeps over the surface of the small beaker in such a manner as to equalise the levels. If the beaker is raised, the liquid still creeps, and drips into the vessel below! This happens till the beaker becomes empty. Once again, this strange phenomenon is connected with the vanishing of the viscosity of liquid helium below 2.2 °K. For more about the superfluid phase transition, see the companion volume entitled *The Many Phases of Matter*.

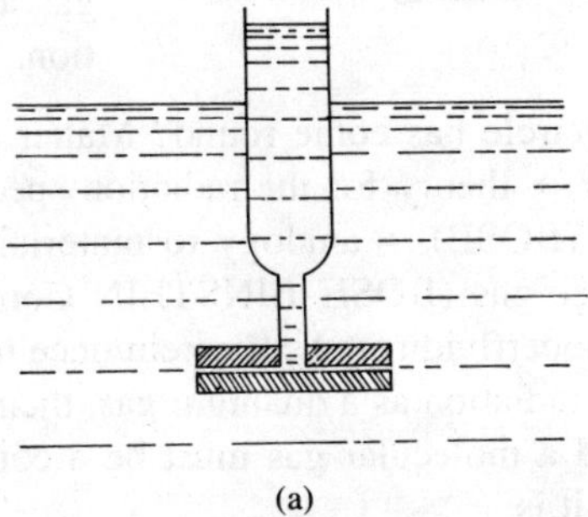

(a)

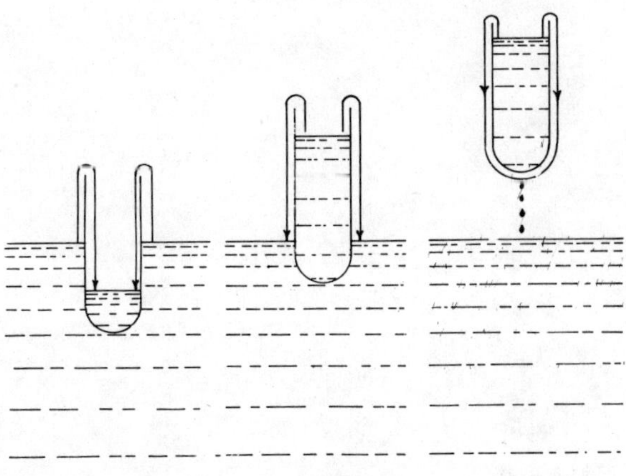

(b)

1915 EINSTEIN:

Bhor atoms Emitted photon filling cavity	——>	Planck's formula again.

1924 BOSE:

Photons Quantum statistics	——>	Planck's law again, but a whole bunch of new and revolutionary ideas, primarily Bose statistics.

1925 EINSTEIN:

Bose statistics Photon analogy	——>	(Ideal) Quantum (Bose) gas, and Bose condensation.

You see how the circle has come round? Matter → emission of radiation from hot matter → theory for the radiation spectrum → photon concept → photon gas (BOSE) → analogy to material gas (EINSTEIN) → condensation of Bose gas (BOSE–EINSTEIN Condensation) → a new property of matter (superfluidity). As Einstein once remarked, "If it is justified to conceive of radiation as a quantum gas, then the analogy between the quantum gas and a molecular gas must be a complete one." Einstein himself showed that it is.

8 *The Later Years*

We return again to the story of Bose. The last time we saw him, he was writing to Einstein enclosing the paper which made him famous. Barely eleven days later Bose wrote again to Einstein, enclosing this time his second paper on radiation (see Chapter 5). He wrote:

Physics Laboratory
Dacca University
Dacca, India
15th June, 1924

Respected Master,

I send herewith another paper of mine for your kind perusal and opinion. I hope my first paper has reached your hands. The result to which I have arrived seems rather important (to me at any rate). You will see that I have dealt with the problem of thermal equilibrium between Radiation and Matter in a different way, and have arrived at a different law for the probability for elementary particles, which seems to have simplicity in its favour. I have ventured to send you the type-written paper in English. It being beyond me to express myself in German (which will be intelligible to you), I shall be glad if its publication in *Zeitschrift fur Physik* or any other German journal can be managed. I myself know not how to manage it. In any case, I shall be grateful if you express your opinion on the papers and send it to me at the above address.

Yours truly,

S.N. Bose

As I mentioned earlier, Einstein got this paper also published, along with a comment which, this time, was somewhat critical. There was no immediate reply to this second letter but Einstein had acknowledged the first letter with a postcard. That card proved useful to Bose.

In early 1924, Bose applied for two years leave from the Dacca University so that he could go to Europe for study and research experience.

Months passed, and the University did not reply. Meanwhile, Bose had written his most famous paper and sent it to Einstein who, as I just told you, sent a post card to Bose in reply. Einstein was already a world-famous scientist, and to get an appreciative letter from him was a great thing. This card solved Bose's leave problem. After seeing it the Vice-Chancellor immediately granted Bose's request for leave.

In October 1924, Bose landed in Europe. First he went to Paris, thinking he would spend a few weeks there before going to Berlin to see Einstein. He did not go directly to Germany because he was not too sure of his ability to speak German; French he was more comfortable with. What started as a few weeks stay in Paris became a year-long one because he met many Indian friends there. They asked him to join them and he enjoyed their company.

Having decided to stay for a while in Paris, Bose thought: "Why don't I learn something about radioactivity from Madame Curie and something about X-rays from Maurice de Broglie [brother of Louis de Broglie, the person who proposed that matter could behave as a particle as well as a wave]?" Through a friend he got an introduction to Madame Curie and went to see her. Bose and Curie spoke to each other in English. Madame Curie was of the view that people working in her lab should know French; otherwise working would not be easy since the workers there did not know English. So she told Bose, "Why don't you go and learn some French first, and then report here?" Bose was too shy to tell her that he already knew French. Instead he said that he could stay in Paris only for six months. He was hinting that he was more interested in Physics than in French. In reply Madame Curie cautioned him not to hurry and advised him to concentrate on the language first. She told Bose about another Indian student in her laboratory who was having problems since he did not know French. After this interview, Bose lost interest in working in Madame Curie's laboratory.

He had better luck with Maurice de Broglie from whom he learnt many techniques in X-ray spectroscopy and X-ray crystallography.

Meanwhile, Bose wrote again to Einstein, this time from Paris. By this time the first paper he had sent to Einstein had appeared in print. He wrote:

17 Rue du Sommerard
Paris V^{e}
26-10-1924

Dear Master,

My heartfelt gratitude for taking the trouble of translating the paper yourself and publishing it. I just saw it in print before I left

India. I have also sent you about the middle of June a second paper entitled, "Thermal equilibrium in the Radiation Field in the presence of Matter."

I am rather anxious to know your opinion about it, as I think it to be rather important. I don't know whether it will be possible also to have this paper published in *Zeitschrift fur Physik*.

I have been granted leave by my university for 2 years. I have arrived just a week ago in Paris. I don't know whether it will be possible for me to work under you in Germany. I shall be glad, however, if you will grant me the permission to work under you, for it will mean for me the realization of a long-cherished hope.

I shall wait for your decision as well as your opinion of my second paper here in Paris.

If the second paper has not reached you by any chance, please let me know. I shall send you the copy I have with me.

With respects,

Yours sincerely,

S.N. Bose

This time, Einstein sent a reply. It contained some references to Bose's second paper.

Berlin W. 30
3 November 1924

Dr. Ś. Bose
17, Rue du Sommerard
Paris.

Dear Colleague:

Thank you sincerely for your letter of 26 October. I am glad that I shall have the opportunity soon of making your personal acquaintance. Your papers have already appeared sometime ago. Unfortunately the reprints have been sent to me instead of you. You may have them at any time. I am not in agreement with your basic principle concerning the probability of interaction between radiation and matter, and have given the reasons in a remark which has appeared together with your paper. Your principle is not compatible with the following two conditions:

1) The absorption coefficient is independent of the radiation density.

2) The behaviour of a resonator in a radiation field should follow from the statistical laws as a limiting case.

We may discuss this together in detail when you come here.
With kind regards,

Yours

A. Einstein

When Bose received this letter, he was disappointed. But he began to think deeply about the objections Einstein had raised, and in January 1925 wrote as follows:

17 Rue du Sommerard
Paris V^e
27th January 25

Respected Master,

I received your kind note of 3rd November in which you mentioned your objections against the elementary law of probability. I have been thinking about your objections all along and so did not answer immediately. It seems to me there is a way out of this difficulty, and I have written down my ideas in the form of a paper which I send under a separate cover. It seems that the hypothesis of negative *Einstrahlung* stands, which, as you have yourself expressed, reflects the classical behaviour of a resonator fluctuating field. But the additional hypothesis of a spontaneous change, independent of the state of the field, seems to me not necessary. I have tried to look at the radiation field from a new standpoint and have sought to separate the propagation of quantum of energy from the propagation of electromagnetic influence. I seem to feel vaguely that some such separation is necessary if quantum theory is to be brought in line with Generalised Relativity Theory.

The views about the radiation-field, which I have ventured to put forward, seem to be very much like what Bohr has recently expressed in May *Phil. Mag.* 1924. But it is only a guess, as I cannot say honestly to have exactly understood all he means to say, about virtual fields and virtual oscillators.

I am rather anxious to know your opinion about it. I have shown it to Professor Langevin here and he seems to think it interesting and worth publishing.

I cannot exactly express how grateful I feel for your encouragement and the interest you have taken in my papers. Your first post card came at a critical moment and it has more than any other made this sojourn to Europe possible for me. I am thinking of going to Berlin at the end of this winter, where I hope to have your inestimable help and guidance.

Yours sincerely,

S.N. Bose

You will notice in this letter that Bose mentions having attempted an answer to Einstein's criticism in the form of a paper. The French scientist Langevin to whom Bose showed the manuscript thought the paper was worth publishing, but somehow, that paper was never published.

Meanwhile, Bose made plans to go to Berlin in October (of 1925) and meet the great master. Bose of course wanted to do much more than making a mere courtesy call to pay his respects. He actually wanted to work with Einstein, and the chances for that seemed good since Einstein was not only showing some interest in Bose's work but had in fact published a sequel to Bose's paper (i.e., the paper which predicted Bose condensation—recall Chapter 7).

When Bose finally arrived in Berlin he was disappointed because Einstein was out of town. But it was only a short absence, and at last the two met. Bose later recalled that "the meeting was most interesting." Einstein asked all kinds of questions about how he (i.e., Bose) got the idea for a new statistics, what he thought about its significance, etc. Bose then found that Einstein had moved on to a new topic namely the unification of the electromagnetic and the gravitational fields (see Box 8.1). So, working with Einstein (that is on problems of statistics) no longer seemed possible. Nevertheless, he decided to spend some time in Berlin as many famous scientists were working there at that time. May be, like in Paris, he could learn a few things. Einstein gave Bose a letter of introduction, and this immediately opened many doors.

Box 8.1 During the last hundred years or so, physicists have been in relentless pursuit of the basic building blocks of matter and the basic forces that bind them. As far as the latter are concerned, there are four of them:

1. Gravitational force
2. Electromagnetic force
3. Weak force
4. Strong force

As you probably know, the gravitational force was discovered by Newton. It is quite feeble actually, but since it can reach out to the farthest corners of the Universe, it really dominates the cosmos. Like gravity, the electromagnetic force is also long-ranged. The weak and the strong forces were discovered during this century. Both are very short-ranged, and do not act beyond distances of the order of 10^{-13} cm. The weak force is responsible for radioactive decay while the strong force binds the particles within the nucleus.

People have always wondered whether these different forces are related to each other in some manner. From about 1920 onwards, Einstein spent all his time trying to unite gravity and electromagnetism, but he did not succeed. In the late sixties / early seventies period, Salam, Weinberg and Glashow succeeded in tying up the weak and the electromagnetic force into one comprehensive force called the *electroweak force*. People are now trying to marry the electroweak force to the strong force and when that is done, the next step naturally would be to bring in gravity also. What it all means is that the four forces we now know are probably different aspects of the same unified force—*avatars* if you like! Does such a unified super grand-daddy force exist or did it ever exist? Well, it is believed that it did exist in the early Universe, meaning that it existed till the Universe attained the age of 10^{-40} sec or so, after which time it (i.e., the unified force) fragmented in stages into the "pieces" or the different forces we now see. If a unification as described above is to be demonstrated in the laboratory, then the energy required for that would be astronomical. In short, it can never be demonstrated. But the unification could probably be *inferred* from tell-tale remnants or evidence surviving from the early Universe.

Just around this time, Heisenberg's papers on quantum mechanics appeared and naturally everyone, Einstein included, was very excited. Since Bose used to meet Einstein regularly, they discussed these developments. As Bose later said, "He wanted me to try to see what the statistics of light-quanta and the transition probabilities of radiation would look like in the new theory [i.e., quantum mechanics]."

Sometime during the latter half of 1926, Bose returned to Dacca. It is curious that although he stayed nearly two years in Europe (during which period physics was in a turmoil and became really exciting), Bose did not publish a single scientific paper. This seems quite strange. Far away in Calcutta and Dacca where facilities were few and communications poor, he had earlier produced a steady stream of papers. Now he was in Europe where there were excellent libraries and where he could meet and discuss with many active people who were working on so many things. And yet Bose never seemed to have completed any piece of work to the point of publishing it. I am very sure Bose was busy reading, absorbing and doing things, for his was a keen and alert mind. And yet this apparent inactivity. Why? I don't have any answers.

Before his return home, his friends told him that he should apply for a professorship at Dacca. But there was a problem. A Professor was usually expected to have a doctorate degree and Bose did not have one. His friends said, "Don't worry, you are famous now and you know Einstein. Get a letter of recommendation from him." Bose therefore went to Einstein and requested him for such a letter. Einstein was most surprised. In Europe things were not done that way. If a person was good, he got the job and a person's ability was judged by the work he had

Dacca. No wonder NPL requested Bose to give a Krishnan Memorial Lecture (delivered every year by an eminent scientist either from India or abroad). Ending his lecture Bose said:

> It is a perpetual challenge to the Indian genius as to how, even though the country is endowed with such natural resources, even though the country has had such a brilliant history, why it continues to remain third rate inspite of so many resources and so much manpower. Well, gentleman, I stop here with these questions asked to our young men.

Think about it!

done. Bose had done excellent work and so why did he need a letter from someone else? Anyway he gave the recommendation but it did not seem to have the desired effect because Dacca University offered the Professor's job not to Satyen Bose but another scientist from Calcutta named D.M. Bose. Luckily for Satyen, D.M. Bose rejected the offer and so finally he could become the Professor.

From 1926 to 1945 Bose remained in Dacca but scientific papers now became rather infrequent events. He dabbled in many things and published the odd paper or two from time to time, quite unlike active workers who usually concentrate in one area, churn out papers and try to become authorities in that field. In Bose's case, his interest shifted from one problem to another. As he later recalled, "On my return to India, I wrote some papers. I did something on statistics and then again on relativity theory, a sort of mixture, a medley. They were not so important. I was really not *in* science any more. I was like a comet, a comet which came once and never returned again."

In 1945, Bose returned to Calcutta to become the Khaira Professor of Physics in Calcutta University. This was one of the professorships instituted by Sir Ashutosh Mookerjee. Bose retired from Calcutta university in 1956 and went to Santiniketan. You might remember that Santiniketan was founded by poet Rabindranath Tagore. Bose and Tagore knew each other, and in fact Tagore had dedicated his book *Visva Parichay* (Introduction to the World of Science) to S.N. Bose. Santiniketan had by now been granted University status and was called the Visva-Bharati University. Bose was to start the teaching of science, besides initiating scientific research in this new University. But old-timers at Santiniketan were upset. They perhaps feared that science would contaminate the arts and did not take kindly to Bose and his efforts. Bose was quite disappointed and returned to Calcutta in 1958. That year he was appointed National Professor. He held this position until his death sixteen years later.

The inspiration of Bose's life was of course Albert Einstein. It is said that when Bose heard of Einstein's death, he wept. While Einstein was a hero, particularly in science, the person whom Bose most revered was the Buddha. This is interesting because Raman also once declared how moved and influenced he was by the life and teachings of the Buddha.

In later years, Bose became actively interested in popularising science and therefore took to writing on science and about science in Bengali. He lived in semi-retirement. Describing it, a friend wrote, "As you enter the sitting-cum-living room, you notice the untidiness, books and magazines strewn all over and stacked willy-nilly on tables, book racks and window sills. Chairs of odd sorts placed for visitors. A wardrobe against a wall, a bedstead, an *esraj* (a musical instrument on which Bose played well) kept on a stand in the corner. On the walls hang framed photo-enlargements of Tagore, Einstein, Mahalanobis, Niren Roy (friend and pupil) and of a group of his friends who used to assemble in a park near his house after college hours. And you see cats. Lots of them. He loves his cats as he does his *esraj*. But you may find him absorbed working on his old love—mathematics. When he hears your footsteps, he looks up endearingly. You pay your respects and tell him what you have come for. A benign smile lights up his face. He helps you over your problem, whatever it may be. You take your leave. You go out of the dishevelled room wrapped in a glow of kindness and warmth. He is a tall scientist; the humanist in him stands even taller."

In January 1974, the Calcutta University organised an international seminar in honour of S.N. Bose. Many leading scientists from all over the world came for the seminar. Bose was present. He was asked to say a few words. He tried to speak standing but had difficulty. He therefore delivered his address seated. He concluded by saying:

> Well, after all, if one has lived through so many years of struggle, and if at the end he finds that his work has been appreciated, he feels that he does not need to live long.

Prophetic words it seemed, for Bose passed away soon after, on 4th February 1974. Bose was no more but Bosons were there for ever.

I think the best way of ending this narrative is to quote what Bose said at the end of his Krishnan Memorial Lecture delivered at the National Physical Laboratory, Delhi. I should perhaps say here a few words about K.S. Krishnan. He was one of Raman's best students, and closely involved with the events leading to the discovery of the Raman effect in 1928. Soon after that he went to Dacca where he was a Reader in the University till he returned to Calcutta around 1933 to become the first Mahendralal Sircar Professor in the Indian Association for the Cultivation of Science. By that time Raman had left Calcutta for Bangalore to become the Director of the Indian Institute of Science. So Krishnan, you may say, stepped into Raman's shoes. Later he moved to Allahabad and, after Independence, became the Founder-Director of the National Physical Laboratory (NPL). Krishnan was not only an excellent physicist but also a great scholar. He was universally loved, and was much admired by Jawaharlal Nehru. In fact, Nehru once said that he would rather be the Director of NPL than be the Prime Minister! That showed Nehru's reverence for science.

Bose and Krishnan knew each other well in Calcutta as well as in

Index

Note: Page numbers in brackets refer to illustrations.